Records Management for Museums and Galleries

CHANDOS
INFORMATION PROFESSIONAL SERIES

Series Editor: Ruth Rikowski
(E-mail: Rikowskigr@aol.com)

Chandos' new series of books is aimed at the busy information professional. They have been specially commissioned to provide the reader with an authoritative view of current thinking. They are designed to provide easy-to-read and (most importantly) practical coverage of topics that are of interest to librarians and other information professionals. If you would like a full listing of current and forthcoming titles, please visit www.chandospublishing.com or e-mail wp@woodheadpublishing.com or telephone +44 (0) 1223 499140.

New authors: we are always pleased to receive ideas for new titles; if you would like to write a book for Chandos, please contact Dr Glyn Jones on e-mail gjones@chandospublishing.com or telephone +44 (0) 1993 848726.

Bulk orders: some organisations buy a number of copies of our books. If you are interested in doing this, we would be pleased to discuss a discount. Please contact e-mail wp@woodheadpublishing.com or telephone +44 (0) 1223 499140.

Records Management for Museums and Galleries

An introduction

CHARLOTTE BRUNSKILL
AND
SARAH R. DEMB

CP
CHANDOS
PUBLISHING

Oxford Cambridge New Delhi

Chandos Publishing
Hexagon House
Avenue 4
Station Lane
Witney
Oxford OX28 4BN
UK
Tel: +44 (0) 1993 848726
E-mail: info@chandospublishing.com
www.chandospublishing.com
www.chandospublishingonline.com

Chandos Publishing is an imprint of Woodhead Publishing Limited

Woodhead Publishing Limited
80 High Street
Sawston, Cambridge CB22 3HJ
UK
Tel: +44 (0) 1223 499140
Fax: +44 (0) 1223 832819
www.woodheadpublishing.com

First published in 2012

ISBNs:
978-1-84334-637-1 (print)
978-1-78063-291-9 (online)

Typeset by Domex e-Data Pvt. Ltd.
Printed in the UK and USA.

Contents

List of figures

Acronyms

BS	British Standard
DPA	Data Protection Act
EDRMS	electronic document and records management systems
EIR	Environmental Information Regulations
EU	European Union
FOIA	Freedom of Information Act
ICO	Information Commissioner's Office
ISAD(G)	General International Standard for Archival Description
IT	information technology
LGA	Local Government Act
NAGPRA	Native American Graves Protection and Repatriation Act
NDPB	non-departmental public body
NMDC	National Museum Directors Conference
PRA	Public Records Act
PRO	Public Record Office
SCAM	Standing Conference on Archives in Museums
TNA	The National Archives

Acknowledgements

We are indebted to the many museum professionals with whom we have worked; to the authors of *Museum Archives: An Introduction* (ed. Deborah Wythe), who set the bar high for this type of publication; and to our own institutions, which have supported our decision to write this book. We are particularly grateful to Alan Crookham, Victoria Lane, Christopher Marsden, Oona Parades and Samira Teuteberg, whose advice and expertise proved invaluable to the finished manuscript.

Sarah would like to thank Claire Sussums for conversations which (often inadvertently) contributed to the book's content; her co-contributors to the Wythe volume and the Society of American Archivists' staff, who encouraged this follow-up book from the other side of the Atlantic; and Connie and Alan Demb, staunch supporters from the very beginning.

Charlotte would like to thank James and Freddie for providing support and inspiration.

Preface

The idea for this book was partially born out of a unique project that included provision of training on records management to museums in the Greater London area.[1] The project demonstrated a widespread need for some sustainable guidance on the subject. Apart from the occasional article, MA dissertation and relevant chapter in *Museum Archives: An Introduction* (Wythe, 2004), little has been written about records management in a museum environment. Not only do information specialists face unique challenges in the museum world, but it is not uncommon for records management concerns to be the responsibility of individuals who have limited experience in the field.

This book addresses that gap. It explores the principles and practice of records management in the specific context of the museum environment. With the exception of Chapter 4 – which focuses specifically on British legislation – the book provides scalable solutions that are relevant to museums everywhere, regardless of size, function or status. The practices discussed are applicable to public (local authority and national), regimental, charitable, university and privately funded museums. They are also relevant regardless of record format, and for that reason paper and electronic records requirements are discussed together. Readers may be experienced information specialists new to the sector, or established museum staff who have been made responsible for managing some or all of an organisation's records. This book is useful across the museum and gallery spectrum.

Note

1. See links to the Renaissance London Information and Records Management Project in Chapter 8.

About the authors

Charlotte Brunskill is archivist and records manager at the Paul Mellon Centre for British Art (sister institution to the Yale Center for British Art in New Haven, CT). Before joining the Paul Mellon Centre in February 2011 she spent seven years at the National Portrait Gallery, where she was responsible for establishing, from scratch, a comprehensive records management and archive programme. She previously worked in a similar capacity at the University of Westminster and the National Gallery. She has been an active member of the National Museums and Galleries Archivist & Records Managers Group, and has published a number of articles and taught records management principles and practice for the London Museums Hub. She holds a master's degree in archive administration and records management from University College London, where she was awarded the Sir Hilary Jenkinson prize for the most outstanding student.

Sarah R. Demb is the first records manager at the Museum of London, where she is also responsible for the museum's institutional archive. Prior to that she was records management adviser to the London Museums Hub, which delivered training and guidance to smaller museums across the region, and previously spent six years as archivist and records manager for the Peabody Museum of Archaeology & Ethnology at Harvard University and the National Museum of the American Indian at the Smithsonian Institution. She has lectured on an international basis on museum archive and records management issues, and also worked in international development, helping to raise capacity in government records management. Sarah has published a variety of articles and papers, and contributed four chapters to the Society of American Archivists' *Museum Archives: An Introduction* (2004). She holds a master's degree in library and information science (with a specialisation in archival enterprise) from the University of Texas at Austin.

The history of record keeping in the UK museum and gallery sector

Charlotte Brunskill

Abstract: Outlines the development of records management in the UK museum sector, international legislative catalysts and record-keeping standards; defines record-keeping roles and activities, and types of museum records; and describes the difference between records, archives and collections.

Key words: records, archive, object records, legislation, standards, special collections, institutional records, collections management, business/administration records.

History

Within the museum environment, the value of good records – at least in one regard – has long been recognised. With the notable exception of the British Museum (established in 1753), the majority of national museums and galleries in the United Kingdom were founded in the Victorian era.[1] Local authority museums also have a long history. The general tendency towards reformism and middle-class paternalism of the time prompted both the Museums Act of 1845[2] and the Public Libraries Act of 1850, which together stimulated an enormous growth in museums in towns with a population of more than 10,000 people. Collections given to local communities by both charitable societies and individuals were housed in civic buildings. As a direct result, many museums and galleries were founded, including those in Exeter, Brighton, Nottingham, Liverpool, Wolverhampton, Birmingham, Aberdeen, Sheffield, Leeds and Preston.[3] In Scotland the legal framework for local authority museums also dates from this period. The Public Libraries (Consolidation) Act 1887 gave local authorities the power to establish museums and galleries. Alongside collecting objects, many of these museums acted as archival repositories, housing important collections of papers and documents.

It was also at this time that record keeping became an established discipline. The Public Record Office Act was passed in 1838 to reform the keeping of public records, which were being held, sometimes in poor conditions, in a variety of places. Although it initially applied only to legal documents, by the 1840s the papers and documents of government departments were also accepted for permanent preservation. This arrangement was legalised by an order in Council issued in 1852. A purpose-built repository to house the material was constructed between 1851 and 1858. Although it functioned primarily as a repository for the records of central government, record keeping became an important activity in most public offices. Clerks were employed specifically to create and maintain good records.

In the museum environment, the focus of this record-keeping effort was centred almost exclusively on the 'object'. The role of museums was to collect objects according to their subject areas or collecting policies, and thereafter to identify/catalogue, preserve, interpret and present these to the public. The staff employed to carry out this work, keepers, directors and curators, were well aware they needed to document their collections. Indeed, record keeping was seen as an extension of curatorial activity, and was often carried out meticulously. The combined effect of this Victorian obsession with record keeping and the curatorial focus on *documenting objects* helped ensure that most museum archives from this era contain a reasonably good record of activity from the early years of their history, albeit collection-focused.

As museums expanded in the twentieth century, record-keeping activities concerned with the collection began to grow. While curators remained responsible for creating research and interpretation-related records, the task of documenting objects became the preserve of a new post: the registrar. As well as recording the acceptance of objects into the collection, the role of the registrar was to document any movement of those objects within and outside of the institution. By the 1970s registrar posts (sometimes also called collections manager posts) began to be introduced in the sector. They are now commonplace in most large museums and galleries.

By 1991 object documentation was a formally recognised core museum function: many institutions now employed whole departments to carry out this work, and further steps were taken to develop and refine the discipline. An impetus to standardise practice across institutions (partly driven by developments in information technology) led to the development of SPECTRUM, the UK museum documentation standard. The purpose of SPECTRUM is to establish 'a common understanding of good practice for museum documentation' (Collections Trust, 2008: 21). The standard was compiled as a collaborative effort by over 100 practising museum professionals. When it was published in 1994 it identified all the functions common to museums and established the procedures and information required to manage these functions effectively. It was a huge achievement and proved invaluable to those in registrar or collections management roles. SPECTRUM is now accepted as the UK and international standard for collections management. In its third edition, it is published by the Collections Trust as an open standard on behalf of the libraries, archives and museums sector.

Although SPECTRUM focuses squarely on documenting museum objects, it does contain some information of use to records managers, or those concerned with general record keeping in a museum environment. By identifying activities familiar to museums, it is possible to extrapolate the types of record series that may be created and determine something of their relative value. By including statements like 'documentation is essential for any organisation which holds a collection', it hints at the value of good record keeping in general. It also contains specific information of interest to records managers. For example, the section on acquisition determines that:

> the accession register... should be made of archival quality paper and be bound in permanent form. If a computer system is being used, copies of new records should be printed out on archival quality paper using a durable print medium and securely bound at regular intervals. The print-out should be signed and dated, preferably on every page. The original register should be kept in a secure condition, ideally in a fire-proof cabinet. (Ibid.: 72.)

However, for the records manager SPECTRUM is ultimately rather narrow. Throughout its 395 pages, the focus is solely on documentation and other information associated with objects. Museum records in their wider sense are barely mentioned.

Since objects are the *raison d'être* of most museums, this record-keeping bias is wholly understandable. Object records are mission critical; museums simply cannot function without them. In order to conduct everyday business, a museum must have access to records concerning the acquisition, location, conservation, loan and so on of the items in its collection. These records are necessary for staff in all departments to do their jobs. For some of the national museums, keeping object records is a statutory duty. The Museums and Galleries Act 1992 declares that alongside the objects themselves certain museums must keep 'documents relating to those works'.[4] As with the objects, they must care for, preserve and provide access to these documents. This record-keeping effort has produced a plethora of documentation. Along with object files, which may contain records about a whole range of activities concerning items in the collection, a museum is also likely to maintain records detailing wider collections management issues, such as acquisitions or accessions, loans and disposal registers.

Until relatively recently, the value of records related to other museum functions – those documenting wider administrative and business activities – was largely overlooked. For example, records concerning building maintenance, development, finance, staff, exhibitions and projects had always been created, but little consideration had been given to their management beyond this point.

The Public Records Acts of 1958 and 1967, which apply to all national museums and galleries, began to change this. They give public institutions a duty to create, preserve and provide access to the records documenting their activities. The Acts prompted museums to consider the value of their records outside the institution: they were no longer viewed primarily as working tools for staff. As a result, many museums began to retain material that might previously have been destroyed and institutional archives (albeit sometimes unknowingly) were founded. The 1967 Act introduced the '30-year rule', which established a standard period after which records should be transferred to the Public Record Office[5] (PRO) and made available to the public. In the museum environment, this generally meant that records were retained in their entirety – little consideration was given to what might have long-term value and what might be destroyed. There was still no systematic records management.

Under the terms of the Acts, museums and galleries – classed as non-departmental public bodies (NDPBs) – were subject to the same rules as central government. They differed on one significant point: unlike central government, museums and galleries were not required to transfer archive records to the PRO. It was recognised that museums needed their records on site to carry out everyday business. Designated places of deposit, they could keep their own records so long as these were maintained in a manner considered satisfactory by the PRO, which carried out regular inspections to ensure that this was the case. This had a significant impact: allowed to manage their own records, record-keeping practice in museums was far less stringent. Unlike government departments, which often operated centralised filing systems or registries, and carefully managed records from creation to destruction or transfer to the archive, many museums tended to retain their records without due consideration of the process that this should entail.

In the 1980s the PRO began to foster closer relationships with NDPBs. It issued guidance, held meetings and conducted more regular inspections. As a result, there was growing awareness of record-keeping best practice (albeit archive-focused) in the national museum sector.

There is no single piece of archival legislation that requires the provision of archive services at a local or regional level for records that have been created by a relevant administrative body. However, a number of Acts go some way towards safeguarding historical records. The Local Government (Records) Act 1962 confers limited discretionary powers for local authorities to provide certain archive functions, but the focus is primarily on service provision. Section 1(1) of the Act states that 'a local authority may do all such things as appear to it necessary or expedient for enabling adequate use to be made of records under its control'. The Local Government Act 1972 includes recommendations about stewardship. It states that local authorities must 'make proper arrangements with respect to any documents that belong to or are in the custody of the council or any of their officers'.[6] It was not until 1999 that the Department for Communities and Local Government attempted to define 'proper arrangements'. Even with this guidance in place, there was no regulatory or monitoring process to verify compliance. For the many museums run by local authorities there was no imperative to manage records.

The establishment in 1989 of the Standing Conference on Archives in Museums (SCAM) was a significant event. It indicated that museum archives were finally being considered seriously within the sector. SCAM was formed as a partnership of three organisations: the Museums Association, the Society of Archivists[7] and the Association for Independent Museums. Members from each group met regularly to discuss the special problems of managing archives in a museum environment. The ultimate aim was to promote research, training, awareness and cooperation about the issues involved at both national and local levels. In 1990 SCAM published the Code of Practice on Archives for Museums and Galleries in the UK. This offered advice to all museums on managing archives according to professional standards. It also suggested additional sources of assistance.

In 1996 the publication of the General International Standard for Archival Description (ISAD(G)) also helped promote archives in the museum environment. Although British archivists had previously looked to the *Manual of Archival Description* (Cook, 1984) for best practice regarding how to describe archival material, ISAD(G), developed by a committee of the International Council on Archives, addressed a much wider audience. For the first time, individuals responsible for archive materials had internationally accepted guidance on how to catalogue the records in their care. The importance of ISAD(G) to the museum sector was that it helped establish archive management as a distinct discipline and emphasised the separate identity of archives; they were not like museum objects and so must be managed very differently.

Meanwhile, the work of SCAM continued to focus primarily on records selected for permanent preservation. Between 1989 and 2003 it produced five information sheets. The first four concern museum archives; it is only in the final sheet that 'administrative records' are considered (SCAM, 2003). The publication of this guide is significant because it marks a culture shift in the museum sector. For the first time it was recorded that along with documentation about collections, 'most museums create and keep large quantities of other records, such as accounts, building and installation plans, exhibition files and membership records' (ibid.: 1). The sheet also gives a definition of records, explaining that the term is not always clearly understood, and what it might include in a museum environment (ibid.: 2).

The SCAM publication is excellent – it distils the relatively complex issue of records management in a museum environment into nine key clear paragraphs. However, the subjects covered belie the state of record keeping in the sector. Together with useful summaries of key concepts, the guide includes basic advice about how to create intelligible records in the first place. For example, section 3 states that it is a good idea to ensure records are dated and stored in files, rather than as loose documents. Inclusion of this basic type of information clearly demonstrates that, at least in some spheres, record keeping in the museum environment was rudimentary.

Spoliation

Between 1998 and 2000 four significant events[8] highlighted the need for good record keeping. The first of these was the endorsement by 44 governments at the Washington Conference on Holocaust Assets in December 1998 of a statement of principles aimed at redressing one of the wrongs of the Second World War: the *spoliation*[9] of works of art by the National Socialist (Nazi) government.

In the UK, work on spoliation was headed by the National Museum Directors Conference (NMDC), a UK-wide voluntary association of 25 cultural institutions partially funded by central government. In June 1998 the NMDC established a working group to investigate the issues surrounding spoliation, draw up a statement of principles and propose actions for member institutions. The statement was finalised and adopted by the NMDC in November of that year, and presented to the Washington Conference the following month. It included the proposal that each national museum, gallery and library draw up an action plan setting out its approach to research into the issue of provenance. A similar statement was issued by the Museums and Galleries Commission[10] in April 1999, as guidance for non-national museums and galleries and a group of university and local authority museums.

The outcome of these events was that museums, galleries and other cultural institutions in the UK (like their counterparts around the world) were required to undertake detailed research into the provenance of works in their collections in order to identify those with uncertain provenance for the period 1933–1945. To do this, museum staff were required to consult their records. Indeed, the 'statement of principles and proposed actions' endorsed by the Washington Conference makes this point very clearly:

> Principle 2. Relevant records and archives should be open and accessible to researchers, in accordance with the guidelines of the International Council on Archives. (National Museum Directors Conference, 1998)

Over the next few years extensive research was carried out in the records and archives of museums and galleries across the UK. The results are available on the NMDC website: each institution submitted a list of works with uncertain provenance.[11] In total 22 national and 24 non-national museums and galleries took part in the effort; each subjected its object records, accession registers, trustee minutes, curatorial correspondence and other relevant records to scrutiny. It was a nationwide (even international) endeavour that clearly demonstrated to the sector the need for and value of good record keeping.

NAGPRA and museums in the United States

In 1990 the Native American Graves Protection and Repatriation Act (NAGPRA) was passed in the United States. This legislation had a similar impact on the museum sector as the spoliation agreement would do eight years later. Unlike the spoliation agreement, NAGPRA was binding only in the USA, but it had (and continues to have) far-reaching international effects. The NAGPRA legislation mandated that all federal agencies and federally[12] (or partially federally) funded museums return human remains, funerary objects, sacred objects and objects of cultural patrimony in their collections to federally recognised Native American tribes.[13]

In order to do this, museums were obliged to carry out comprehensive inventories within five years which had to 'associate' objects definitely with Native American groups, so they could be published and sent to tribes. In addition to its groundbreaking human rights aspects and the profound shift in Native/non-Native relationships, this complex process pushed both archival and records management to the forefront of museum business functions and left no doubt as to the importance of both object and institutional documentation. The entire process is based on meticulous research by all parties, and records were made equally available to both museum staff and claimants.

Repatriation claims from tribes and native sovereign nations in Canada, Australia and New Zealand followed swiftly, and the repatriation cause was also taken up with non-American museums. This massive undertaking to redress past inequities now seen as unethical will continue for decades to come and has changed the way many museums address their collecting past and interpret their exhibitions, along with their collections documentation and other records. In 2006 the British Museum returned two individuals (their remains in the form of ash bundles) to the Tasmanian Aboriginal

Centre, an act probably unheralded before NAGPRA.[14] In 2009 the Booth Museum in Brighton and Hove announced that it would return Australian aboriginal remains outstanding from a 2005 request.[15]

Between NAGPRA legislation and later spoliation regulations, almost every type of museum in the USA, from local history houses to international art collections, has had to re-evaluate its holdings and its records.

Other legislative catalysts

On 24 October 1998 the European Union (EU) Data Protection Directive (95/46/EC) came into effect in the UK through the Data Protection Act 1998 that received Royal Assent on 16 July. The directive's aims were to protect human rights and freedoms in respect of personal data processing and to facilitate the free flow of data within the EU. By allowing people to request any and all personal data held about them by an organisation, and simultaneously requiring organisations to protect personal data they held from unauthorised access, it had a significant impact on the work of archivists and records managers in the UK. The Act applies to institutions responsible for processing personal data.[16] It therefore encompasses all types of national, local, charity, university and regimental museums.

The 1998 Act replaced the Data Protection Act 1984 and its provisions are much broader in scope. Specifically, while the 1984 Act applied only to data held in electronic form, the new Act was expanded to include manual data held in 'relevant filing systems'. For the museums and galleries sector this was significant: records historically collected for years in paper format – concerning donors, lenders, members, patrons and visitors – all contained personal data and were therefore likely to be affected.

Some of these records were also non-object-related records, so they had traditionally been subject to less rigorous management. The Act forced the sector to move away from its focus on archive records, and to consider how it collected and managed current records and the data they contained. In particular, Principle 5 of the Act, which states that that personal data shall be 'held for no longer than is necessary for the purposes for which they were obtained',[17] meant that disposal of records had to be seriously considered. Records management as a systematic practice was becoming a necessity.

Electronic records

In March 1999 the government published its *Modernising Government* white paper.[18] This visionary document set out the aim that all government departments should be capable of delivering 100 per cent of their public services electronically by 2008. To facilitate this, public institutions were instructed to take steps to ensure that all newly created public records could be stored and retrieved electronically. The National Archives (TNA) led work on this initiative. It published a 'route map and milestones towards electronic records management by 2004',[19] which set out the steps institutions must take. These included:

- conducting an extensive audit of e-records
- compiling an inventory of those records
- establishing appraisal and preservation plans for electronic records
- developing a corporate electronic records management policy.

All national museums and galleries were expected to comply. In short, this document forced the sector to consider the fact that most institutions had limited control over their paper record systems, let alone those in electronic format, and this was a daunting prospect. TNA was responsible for monitoring compliance. This was mostly done through a series of meetings organised by the sector's client manager at TNA. Archivists (and where they existed, records managers) working in the national museums and galleries were invited to report back and share their experiences. As a result, most began to conduct basic e-record audits to identify what records were being created and determine their relationship with those in paper formats. Perhaps most significantly, nearly all started to work closely with their information technology (IT) colleagues.

At the time, TNA promoted the purchase and implementation of electronic document and records management systems. While many central government departments followed this route, these systems were prohibitively expensive for most national museums and galleries. Faced with implementing electronic records management with existing resources, many began to develop corporate file plans and structures: a key feature of good records management programmes. The impact of the *Modernising Government* agenda was significant: it prompted the sector to consider record keeping in its widest sense, encompassing records of all subjects and in all formats.

ISO 15489

The publication in 2001 of 'International Standard ISO 15489-1:2001 Information and documentation – records management' was an important event for the records management profession generally. It was developed in response to a consensus within the records management community to standardise international best practice. Establishing records as a business asset and focusing on the efficiencies achieved by good records management, it provided a considerable driver for the discipline. It is supported by British Standard (BS) PD0025-2:2002 (effective records management, practical implementation of BS ISO 15489, published in 2002), which provides an accessible and practical guide to implementation and is particularly aimed at new or non-professional records managers. Within the museums and galleries sector these standards also helped establish records management as a distinct discipline, just as ISAD(G) had done for archives five years before.

Freedom of Information Act

The most significant event for records management in the public sector, if not in the UK generally, was undoubtedly the passing of the Freedom of Information Act (FOIA) in 2000. The Act applies to national, local authority and university museums. It gives individuals the right to access records held by public institutions. On receipt of a request, institutions have 20 working days to respond. The FOIA effectively replaces the 30-year rule, determining that records should be released to the public unless a specific exemption applies. For the first time, public institutions were legally required to provide access to their current and semi-current records. Those who did not or could not would be investigated by the Information Commissioner's Office (the independent body charged with policing the Act). Institutions whose record-keeping practices were chaotic would find it very difficult to comply.

To prepare public institutions for the Act, the Lord Chancellor issued the Code of Practice on the Management of Records, laid before Parliament on 20 November 2002.[20] Part One of the code is unequivocal: it states in section 5.1 'The records management function should be recognised as a specific corporate programme within an authority and should receive the necessary levels or organisational support to ensure effectiveness'; and again in section 7.1, 'a designated member of staff of appropriate seniority should have lead responsibility for records management within the authority'. The code goes on to outline the basic requirements for managing records creation, review, disposal and archival transfer. Public institutions could no longer avoid it: establishing a robust records management programme was not just common sense, it was mandatory.

The practical implications of the FOIA (and other legislation) are explored in a later chapter, but the deep impact of the Act and the Lord Chancellor's Code of Practice on records management in the museum and galleries sector cannot be overestimated. The code was updated in 2009; the new version (containing, for example, a section headed 'The importance of records management') is even more explicit in advocating the need for good record keeping. A recent survey of ten major national museums and galleries revealed that in 2000 only one employed a records manager; in 2010 seven of the ten had such a post on the payroll.[21] Indeed, the last decade has seen extraordinary developments in the sector: when first introduced, most records management posts were established reluctantly and on a temporary basis. At best they were seen as short-term get-the-job-done project posts, brought in to conduct a one-time survey of record keeping in the institution, establish best practice and ensure compliance with the Act, after which it was thought they would be redundant. At worst they were instigated with the vaguest of remits, simply to 'tick the FOIA box' and deal with the mess. In both cases, museums and galleries were initially unwilling to make a significant investment in records management.

But records managers have begun to prove their worth. Of the ten institutions surveyed, five records management roles in the national museum and gallery sector are now permanent posts (it should be noted that some of these roles are of a dual nature, with responsibility for the institutional archive record). In addition to conducting record surveys, establishing best practice and helping ensure compliance with the FOIA, they are now actively involved in a wealth of activities including managing electronic records and addressing digital sustainability issues.

Significantly, there is a growing understanding of the relationship between records management and the institutional archive. Museum and gallery records are increasingly managed in a seamless fashion, from creation to destruction or transfer to the archive. Archives themselves are regularly exploited as a resource to celebrate anniversaries and promote brand identity in addition to their research function. Most national museums and galleries have now produced institutional histories based on material in the archive. Many have also published texts focusing on particular aspects of that history: archive records do not just tell us about the institution, they help to understand broader questions of social and cultural history. Museums and galleries have long been interested in the archival record; most now recognise that if they want to hold an archive that properly reflects their institutional history, it is vital to have a robust records management programme.

The value of records management in supporting core business is also increasingly acknowledged. Keeping good records informs decision-making and promotes efficiencies, and records managers are emerging as information specialists – a valuable commodity in the museum environment. This is demonstrated by the fact that four out of the seven records management posts noted earlier are located in the directorial/ strategic, rather than research, area of the institution. The impact of the FOIA is far from diminishing; requests received each year are increasing and the resulting transparency in business is slowly filtering through to private institutions. The public now expect openness, regardless of an institution's status.

Records managers themselves have been proactive in developing best practice and promoting excellence in the sector. In 2004 representatives from the National Portrait Gallery, the Tate and the Imperial War Museum produced a generic file plan for museums and galleries. In 2007 an electronic records management working group was formed to discuss issues relevant to museums and galleries and investigate the potential benefits of collaboration.

Through initiatives like the Renaissance London Museum Hub's Information and Records Management Project (started in 2007, and continuing at the time of writing), experience at the national level is further developed, refined and disseminated to non-national and regional museums.[22] The Hub project has been responsible for promoting good practice via guidance materials and training workshops. Although the materials were produced for museums in the London region, they are freely available to any institution.

Work also continues with archive-related guidance materials. In 2006 the Archives in Museums Specialist Skills Network was established. Continuing the work of SCAM, it seeks to support and help those looking after archives within museums. It is open to all and resources are free to download via the Collections Link website.[23]

The last ten years have seen remarkable change: in 2000 museum records management was practically non-existent; now it is a recognised and growing discipline at the national museum and gallery level. For all this progress, however, there is still much work to do. Establishing and maintaining a records management programme in even a moderate-sized institution represent an enormous amount of work, and most museums and galleries are still under-resourced in this area. The roles of archivist and records manager are frequently shared by one post. Although this situation supports the seamless management of records (from creation to destruction or maintenance as an archival record) and is particularly welcome in a museum environment where many core record series (such as object files) are permanently active,[24] this amalgamation of the two disciplines frequently means that neither gets the full attention it deserves. In addition, although sector-specific guidance is beginning to emerge, there is still a great deal to be done before best practice is fully implemented. Electronic records remain an enormous challenge (not just in the museum and gallery sector), but provide an imperative for records management whereby issues regarding obsolescence demand that the sector takes steps now to secure its archives for the future.

Record keeping in museums: roles

Record keeping in the museum environment has a long and complex history (Figure 1.1). It has often been viewed as the preserve of particular staff or section(s) of the institution, and the usual focus has been on records related to objects or those of archival nature. These traditions have left a legacy: the scope of the records manager's role is frequently misunderstood. Re-educating an institution accordingly is a

Figure 1.1 Summary of key developments in the museum and gallery sector

Decade	Object records	Archive records	Records management
Pre-1900s	Majority of UK museums and galleries established with the primary purpose of collecting objects (Museums Act 1845 and Public Libraries Act 1850)	Public Record Office Act 1838 Public Record Office Act 1877	
1900s			
1910s			
1920s			
1930s			
1940s			
1950s		Public Records Act 1958	
1960s		Local Government (Records) Act 1962 Public Records Act 1967	
1970s	Establishment of registrar/collections management posts	Local Government Act 1972	
1980s		Establishment of professional museum archivists in larger museums and galleries

Standing Conference on Archives in Museums (SCAM) | |

Figure 1.1	Summary of key developments in the museum and gallery sector (*cont'd*)		
1990s	Museums and Galleries Act 1992 Publication of SPECTRUM standard, 1994	International Standard of Archival Description (General)	Endorsement of Spoliation Statement of Principles, 1998 Data Protection Act 1998 *Modernising Government* agenda, 1999
2000s			Freedom of Information Act 2000 Establishment of records management in national museums and galleries International Standard ISO 15489-1:2001

significant and important task. To do so effectively, it is necessary to have a clear understanding of the roles and responsibilities common in a museum environment.

While almost everyone in museums has some record-keeping duties, a number of roles have significant responsibilities attached. In small institutions these roles may be distilled into one job. In others they may be undertaken by different staff. In both cases understanding the various approaches to record keeping and identifying the (sometimes subtle) differences between the requirements of each are vital if the records management programme is to be successful.

Records manager

Records management is concerned with managing records from creation to disposal. Traditionally, records managers are responsible for developing and implementing policies and procedures that help manage the daily creation, use and disposal of active and inactive records across the museum. They are concerned with the records produced by staff in the course of their everyday business; the material which is created daily in paper and electronic formats across the museum. Increasingly, this involves working with IT departments or third-party providers to manage e-mail systems and shared drives, as well as social networking (e.g. Web 2.0) applications and website content. When these records have reached the end of their 'life cycle', those identified as having permanent value are transferred to the archive.

Archivist

An archivist is concerned with managing records that have been identified for permanent retention because they have value to future generations. Archival management comprises the accession,[25] processing, cataloguing and research use of and access to records designated as having permanent value to the museum. Archivists also conduct research on the history of the museum and ensure that material continues to be added to the archive, via *internal transfer* from its records management programme and/or *donations* from former staff or others. Some museums can afford to purchase museum records that may have left the museum and appear on the market, but most rely on donations from families of former staff to regain items that have inadvertently walked out of the doors. Museum archivists may be responsible for the institution's own archival records, and/or archive material created by and acquired from external sources. This material is sometimes called 'collected archives' or 'special collections' (see below for a detailed explanation). In some institutions the roles of records manager and archivist are held by different individuals, but in many they are amalgamated into one post.

Registrar/collections manager

Registrars are responsible for asserting intellectual and physical control over objects entering and leaving the museum. They oversee and document the acquisition, accession and disposal of museum objects and do the same for loans in and out of the museum. In museums without registrars, curators are often responsible for registration functions. Depending on the museum's policy, registrars may also accession special collections, or collected archives of other institutions or individuals that come into the institution's physical custody. Accession files, accession registers, object files (sometimes called control files or case files), loans records and collections databases are often maintained by registrars.

Documentation officer

Larger museums may have the luxury of documentation officers, in charge of maintaining and administering collections databases and/or object files. Documentation officers are responsible for ensuring that object information is recorded according to external and internal standards across the entire museum. They may conduct object inventories and ensure that location information in databases is current, and help to develop and apply data standards.

Curator

Curators often carry out a huge range of tasks. Besides researching collections and developing exhibitions, they may also act as registrar, collections manager and/or documentation officer. Some curators are responsible for keeping object and loans files as well as accession registers. Even in large museums, curators often add information to collections management databases as they research object provenance or special subject areas. Curators may also create and keep exhibition files which may later end up in museum archives. They respond to vast numbers of external enquiries about museum collections and objects, and work with press and marketing officers to publicise the museum's exhibits and holdings. Where there is no registrar, curators are often responsible for documenting object loans in and out of the museum.

Information manager

Information managers coordinate information policy and procedure (and sometimes the appropriate staff) across the museum. They ensure that the museum has a consistent and strategic approach to managing and leveraging its myriad information assets, in both electronic and manual (paper) formats. Records management and archives functions often fall under the broader umbrella of information management, as do documentation, registration and special collections.

Record keeping in museums: record types

Museum and gallery records are regularly managed as, or at least perceived as belonging to, the following groups (Figure 1.2).

Figure 1.2 Records of a museum

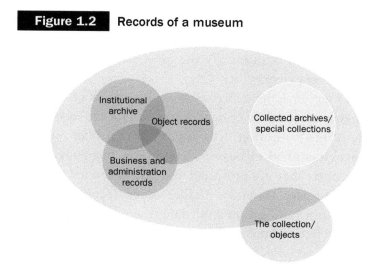

Institutional archive

Object records

Collected archives/ special collections

Business and administration records

The collection/ objects

Collections management records

Collections management records are also called collections *documentation* records. As discussed earlier in this chapter, record keeping in a museum environment has historically focused on the object. Museum staff have long recognised the value of object-related records. These may include accession correspondence and registers used to document the museum's acquisition process. They also include records relating to individual objects themselves and may encompass documentation produced by the activities of acquisition, research, conservation, loan and display. These records may be filed together in an object file or by accession group, or can equally be maintained as a number of separate series.

These records have a high status within the institution. For national museums, this may be concerned with the fact that they have a statutory duty to maintain them as set out in the Museums and Galleries Act 1992. However, this heightened status is not a new phenomenon; object files have long been considered important both because they directly document the collection and because they are created and used by curators, traditionally the most senior staff in the museum environment.

For all museums, these records should be classified as *vital* because they are 'mission critical': necessary for the successful running of the institution. It is important that *vital records* are clearly identified in business continuity and emergency plans to ensure they are protected and prioritised for salvage in the worst-case scenario. Unlike other records, object records do not have an 'expiry' date: they are created and then remain in constant use for as long as the object remains in the collection (which, in most cases, will be for the life of the institution) or until (and even after) it has been deaccessioned. To explain further, they do not move through the stages of the record life cycle in the manner described in Chapter 2. They are created and remain 'active' for the whole of their life. Perhaps most crucially, they have immediate archival status; their value to future generations is recognised at the time of original receipt or creation.

As a result of all the above, collections management records have historically benefited from better management than other museum records. As explored earlier, a great deal of practical guidance exists for collection records (not least SPECTRUM), and the curator, registrar or collections manager post is dedicated in part to ensuring that object records are created and managed effectively. For all of these reasons, collections management records are often seen to exist separately from the rest of the museum's records.

This idea is misleading for records management purposes. Object and collections management/documentation records are no different from any other museum records; they have been created by the museum in the course of its normal business and should be incorporated in the records management programme. This is important, because as 'mission critical' records they must be included in any institution-wide record-keeping initiative, and the rules documenting their management must be clearly established and understood by all staff. Including collections management records in a museum records management programme also allows them to be seen in their widest context, along with all the other records created by the institution – a principle which is at the heart of good archival practice concerning *provenance*.

General business, operational or administrative records

This group comprises the bulk of records created by a museum or gallery. It includes records concerning the following areas of activity.

- *Organising exhibitions* – can include records produced in the course of developing exhibition proposals, borrowing objects for display, managing exhibition spaces, etc.

- *Facilitating learning and access* – can include records produced in the course of developing education programmes, organising lectures and workshops, compiling online learning resources, etc.

- *Governing the museum* – can include records produced in the course of managing the high-level business of the institution, liaising with governing bodies, developing policy and strategy, etc.

- *Managing commercial activities* – can include records produced in the course of hiring the institution as a venue, licensing its assets, producing publications, etc.

- *Developing external relationships* – can include records produced in the course of liaising with the press, developing corporate and individual membership, enhancing community relations, etc.

- *Managing resources* – can include records produced in the course of managing the institution's staff, buildings and grounds, finance, etc., as well as managing information more broadly.

Institutional archive

This group of material comprises the records received and created by the institution, from all areas of activity, selected for long-term or permanent preservation because they have ongoing historical value. A good records management programme identifies archival material and ensures records are transferred to the institutional archive at the appropriate time. The institutional archive is the final and lasting outcome of a good records management programme. Depending on the size and available resources of the institution, the records manager may also be responsible for the archive and vice versa.

Key *record series* likely to become part of a museum or gallery's institutional archive include:

- minutes and papers of the museum's board of trustees
- minutes and papers of other significant committees
- annual reports
- financial accounts
- corporate and business plans
- object files (including acquisition and conservation records)
- accession registers
- loan registers
- exhibition case files
- building records and plans

- research subject files (including correspondence and research notes)
- visitor reports/surveys.

It is worth noting that in a museum environment (particularly where an archive or records management programme has yet to be introduced), the term 'archive' is sometimes applied to compiled histories of the institution (records that have been created or specifically brought together to form an institutional history). Often these records are bound in volume or scrapbook form, and may focus on particularly interesting episodes such as a history of the museum during the Second World War. Although these records may be fascinating, and should undoubtedly form *part* of the institutional archive, they are not the institutional archive itself. They represent a cherry-picked narrative and cannot replace the value of records viewed in their integral context. A true institutional archive preserves records in their original context and allows users to compile their own history. (It is worth bearing in mind that some staff may not appreciate this distinction.)

Institutional archives, although often perceived by the museum as being very separate, are part of the institution's record. They must therefore be considered part of an integrated records management and archive programme, even if more than one staff member or different teams manage these activities.

There are also two groups of records, detailed below, likely to be held by a museum or gallery that are not part of the institutional record.

Special collections

Special collections (sometimes called collected papers or collected archives) include any records created by and acquired from external sources, usually because they support or add value to the institution's main collection.

For example, the Archive of the National Portrait Gallery acquires the papers of portrait artists because these inform an understanding of both the portraits themselves and research into portraiture more generally. Whatever the subject matter and whatever the method of acquisition – donation, gift, purchase or bequest – the key difference is that these records have been acquired from outside the institution and, perhaps more crucially, were not created by the institution in the course of its daily business.

The Museum of London holds two collected archives: the Port and River Archive (including the records of the Port of London Authority) and the Sainsbury Archive (records of the supermarket chain). These archives document the activities of two external organisations, and are held by the Museum of London as collections in their own right – part of the history of London that the museum exists to document and interpret. For these reasons, they are not part of the museum's records management programme.

There may be instances where records have been acquired from external sources but still form part of the institutional archive. For example, in previous years the distinction between the private and working papers of senior staff such as museum directors was often blurred, and as a result these records were frequently taken off site. Museums may later acquire such records posthumously from family members, and these materials should then be added to the institutional archive.

So it is the creator and context of the record rather than *the source of acquisition* that determines whether the material is part of the museum record. Therefore, special collections should not be considered part of a records management programme (although the records that document the *administration* of a special collection will fall under the records management programme).

The object collection

The object collection can include material in any format: paintings, scientific instruments or specimens, photographs, historical and archaeological artefacts and indeed documentary material such as film. The collection comprises whatever the museum collects, preserves, interprets and presents to the public. Many museums also acquire documents for their collections. In these cases, the records are accessioned objects in themselves and should not fall under the records management programme. In many museums, collected objects such as books may overlap with or are managed as part of library collections.

Managing documents as objects is perfectly acceptable if this is how they have been acquired. However, a common practice in some institutions is to transfer museum records into the collection once they are identified as being of particular interest. For example, the National Portrait Gallery's institutional archive contains a series of photographs of staff and other individuals (such as trustees) created in the course of daily gallery business. Some of these feature famous or noteworthy personalities, and the temptation in the past has been for museum staff to remove these from their records series and catalogue them as single items for the collection. This is undesirable. If the record forms part of the museum's institutional record – it was created as a by-product of the everyday activity of the institution, rather than specifically commissioned or acquired for the object collection – it should not be transferred to the collection.

This material must remain with unbroken provenance, in context – that is, among the other records created by the institution – in order to be fully understood. If an institution manages its records appropriately the material should be accessible no matter who is responsible for it or where it is stored.

The overall picture

So, museums and galleries *keep records of all types or formats*, in a *variety of contexts* and according to *different management regimes*. This can be confusing – what distinguishes one record from the next, and which should be included in a records management programme? Crucial to this decision is the creator: if a record was created or received by the institution in the course of its everyday business, it should be incorporated in the records management programme. This includes records concerning the collection (object files, accession registers, etc.) as well as records from all other areas of museum business (exhibitions, press, education and so on).

The records manager, or person with records management responsibility, may not have physical custody of all these records or day-to-day responsibility for maintaining them, but that person *must* have responsibility for managing them on an intellectual level. This includes advising staff on how to organise and store records, helping to determine records' final disposition or transfer to the archive and developing overarching policies to manage these activities. Records management should constitute a corporate, museum-wide view: it should encompass all records created by the institution, regardless of custodian, format or subject matter.

Notes

1. For example, the National Gallery in 1824, the V&A in 1852, the National Portrait Gallery in 1856, the National Gallery of Scotland in 1859, the Natural History Museum in 1881 and the National Gallery of British Art (now Tate) in 1897.
2. The full title is An Act for Encouraging the Establishment of Museums in Large Towns.
3. For dates of establishment see Taylor (1999: 100).

4. Museums and Galleries Act 1992, section 2(1)–(3).
5. In 2003 the Public Record Office merged with the Historical Manuscripts Commission to become The National Archives.
6. Local Government Act 1972, section 224.
7. In June 2010 the Society of Archivists merged with the National Council on Archives and the Association of Chief Archivists in Local Government to become the Archives and Records Association.
8. The four significant events are the endorsement of a statement of principles by 44 governments at the Washington Conference on Holocaust Assets, the Data Protection Act 1998, the *Modernising Government* agenda in 1999 and the Freedom of Information Act 2000.
9. Spo·li·a·tion: n.
(i) the seizing of things by force
(ii) the seizure or plundering of neutral ships at sea by a belligerent power in time of war
(iii) the alteration or destruction of a document so as to make it invalid or unusable as evidence.
Encarta World English Dictionary.
10. In 2005 the Museums and Galleries Commission became the Museums, Libraries and Archives Council. In 2010 the body was abolished: responsibility for museums and libraries was passed to the Arts Council England and responsibility for archives to TNA.
11. See *www.culturalpropertyadvice.gov.uk/spoliation_reports* (accessed: 1 April 2010).
12. 'Federal' in this case equates to national. The Smithsonian Institution museums do not fall under NAGPRA, but are bound by similar repatriation regulations. In all museums, non-archaeological objects or 'objects of cultural patrimony' did not fall under the same deadlines.
13. For a more detailed outline of the process, see Wythe (2004: 182–4).
14. See *www.britishmuseum.org/the_museum/news_and_press_ releases/statements/human_remains/repatriation_to_tasmania .aspx* (accessed: 7 April 2010).
15. See *www.brighton-hove-rpml.org.uk/Museums/Documents/ policy%20documents/Note%20on%20return%20of%20Ind*

igenous%20Australian%20Human%20Remains.doc (accessed: 7 April 2010).

16. Under the terms of the Act, personal data are defined as information which relates to a living individual who can be identified. Processing includes obtaining, holding, retrieving and altering data. The definition is very wide and therefore it is difficult to identify any data functions an organisation might carry out that would not be classed as processing.

17. Data Protection Act 1998, Schedule, Part I, Principle 5.

18. See *http://archive.cabinetoffice.gov.uk/moderngov/download/modgov.pdf* (accessed: 1 April 2010).

19. See *http://pdfdatabase.com/download/public-record-office-routemap-and-milestones-for-electronic-records-management-by-2004-pdf-15598557.html* (accessed: 31 March 2010).

20. See *www.justice.gov.uk/downloads/guidance/freedom-and-rights/foi-section-46-code-of-practice.pdf* (accessed: 31 March 2010).

21. Unpublished survey by authors, April 2010.

22. The London Museums Hub is a consortium of regional museums funded by Renaissance London – the Museums, Libraries and Archives Council's groundbreaking initiative to invest in and transform the country's museums.

23. See *www.collectionslink.org.uk* (accessed: 31 March 2010).

24. Permanently active records are those that have been identified as having archival value but remain in everyday use by their creators.

25. For more information on the differences between accessioning objects into the museum and records into the archives, see Wythe (2004: 96–100).

2

Records management basics

Sarah R. Demb

Abstract: Explores and defines the terms, concepts and ideas key to records management: records, records and information management, records life cycle, records continuum, archival management and records series. Outlines the benefits of records management.

Key words: evidence, records and information management, records life cycle, records continuum, archival management, records series, corporate asset.

Introduction

Museums are information businesses. They exist to collect, generate, interpret and disseminate information about their collections, their social and historical contexts and wider trends in society. *Information management* addresses ownership of information within the organisation, intellectual property rights and policies/procedures regarding data, records and capture and dissemination systems. It encompasses all information, data and records created and managed by an institution. *Records management* is an important stream or subset of activities within this information environment. It enables museums to organise much of the information they hold. Records are *corporate assets* which should be maximised and protected.

Before implementing a records management programme, it is important to understand some basic definitions.

What is a record?

A record provides *evidence* of a transaction, activity, decision or event; it may need to be proven or referenced over the medium or long term[1] and can exist in any format (e.g. paper, electronic, microfilm, magnetic and optical media, photographs, slides or other images). Thus records include paper correspondence, word-processed documents, text messages, e-mails, web forms, digital CCTV footage and audio and video recordings, to name a few examples.[2]

Records may have *multiple values* that can be characterised as:

- *administrative or informational*: records needed to carry out work on a daily basis by their creators or others
- *evidential*: records that provide proof over time of decisions made, transactions carried out and events which take place
- *financial and legal*: closely related to evidential value, ensuring compliance with finance and human resources regulations and legislative requirements related to a variety of subjects, including health and safety, freedom of information and data protection
- *historical/research*: some records have long-term value and are identified for permanent preservation because of their interest to future generations; the business or institutional archives of museums are often used by academics, genealogists, family historians and the museum itself.

It is also helpful to consider some of the characteristics of the record as identified by the British pioneer of archival management, Hilary Jenkinson, in the early part of the twentieth century, although it is worth noting that in a digital context some of them, such as neutrality and uniqueness, might not go unchallenged by today's archivists.[3]

- *Neutrality* – records are a means and by-product of work, not the work itself, and therefore are impartial. Records are not created solely as evidence of work or for posterity, but as part of the processes necessitated by an organisation's work. Therefore, they become impartial evidence of those processes.

- *Authenticity* – records are credible and reliable because they are created or received by staff as part of the documented business processes agreed by the organisation to carry out its work.

- *Institutional provenance and context (robustness)* – very few records stand on their own. They are a product of business processes and as such are interrelated. They tell the story of the work conducted by the organisation in a way that no single document could do and no secondary source could evidence. A robust record has a history that can be traced to its records series (described below) and ultimately to the *records group*, or *fonds*,[4] of which it is a part. In the world of electronic records, explicit audit trails prove the robustness of the record.

- *Uniqueness* – the circumstances under which the record is created make it significant and unique.

What is records management?

Records management is the systematic process of implementing a set of tools and guidance that enable an organisation to locate and retrieve the right information in the right format by the right person at the right time at the lowest possible cost, with the least amount of effort (Wythe, 2004: 112), within the local legal and regulatory environment. More traditional definitions of the term incorporate the concept of the *records life cycle*, which is explained later in this chapter. The main tools used to implement records management are the *policy*, *file plan* and *retention schedule* (discussed in detail in Chapter 7).

Organisations such as museums benefit from implementing records management because it:

- *increases efficiency* by avoiding reliance on individual idiosyncrasies of organising information – records are organised according to a corporate/agreed structure and are therefore more readily available to staff
- *saves time and money* by ensuring that staff do not lose track of, recreate or store duplicate information
- ensures that *corporate memory* is retained, so that staff transitions do not necessitate 'reinventing the knowledge wheel'
- facilitates *compliance with legislation* because records are maintained as evidence of transactions and managed in accordance with statutory responsibilities
- protects and enhances an organisation's *reputation* via the resulting audit trails which make the organisation more accountable and transparent – risk is managed in the understanding that a full record is kept on what information is held, where and by whom.

In other words, a lack of proper records management results in the following problems common across organisations:

- inability to locate records and information quickly and efficiently
- duplication of information (holding multiple copies of the same record)

- confusion about which person or post holds the official record

- confusion about what to keep, what to throw away and when to do so

- non-compliance with legal requirements related to records keeping, such as the FOIA and data protection statutes.

The 'difference' between archives and records management

Traditionally, an institutional *archive* comprises those materials created and received by an organisation in the course of everyday business that have been *identified as having permanent value*, whether for legal, evidential or research purposes. Without this designation (which should be assigned according to sector-standard processes and procedures – see Chapters 5 and 7), materials are not 'archival'; they are merely *inactive* or possibly (but not always) old.

The exception that occurs in museums and other heritage organisations, such as libraries and stand-alone archives, tends to be collections documentation, which is continuously used for both the purpose for which it was originally created by those same creators and by others over time for research, and which has permanent archival value. Collections documentation such as accession files is therefore *permanently active records*.

Archival management standards and practice exist to ensure that records which have permanent value are arranged, described, catalogued, preserved and accessed over time.

The expanded second edition of the Society of American Archivists' *Museum Archives: An Introduction* (2004) is a practical step towards redressing the not-so-benign neglect of archives. It is a widely known trope to characterise archive material or archives as 'dusty', due to the fact that there is a tendency to forget where the materials came from in the first place. 'Dusty' archives are those records that are of permanent value but that are not used and, almost more importantly, are unmanaged.

However, archives and records management are intricately linked. Records management principles are designed to help manage the records we create, receive, use and dispose of in day-to-day work across the myriad functions of organisations like museums. In the main, archival materials are used for purposes different to those for which they were originally created, even when the users are the same staff who created the records. Archival management, as detailed in Wythe's volume (ibid.), outlines how to care for those records at that stage of their 'life'.

Arguably, in the 'records continuum' described below archival management is a subset – or a major component – of records management; certainly, many museums assign responsibility for both archives and records management functions to one person. This is not just a money-saving decision; it is also because both jobs require a similar skill set which allows for a holistic view and management of an institution's records. There are also important intellectual and functional reasons for doing so. As discussed in Chapter 1, historically museums tended to focus on one narrow band of records management – that of managing the documentation of object collections. This situation often resulted in a paucity of material in the museum archive regarding non-collections-related activities, leaving organisations with an incomplete picture of the institution's values, mission and history; a gap in its own documentary heritage.

Wythe partially defines the function of the museum archive[5] as the keeper of institutional records and the research centre through which they are accessed (ibid.: 9).

She also points out that the function of the museum archive is twofold: it is a valuable resource for both museum staff and external researchers (ibid.: 11).

This book focuses on an earlier stage – managing records for the purposes for which they are created – but especially in the electronic environment of the museum's record keeping, the continuum approach is more relevant and useful.

Basic records management concepts

The records life cycle

Many records managers find the idea of the records 'life cycle' useful (Figure 2.1). The life-cycle concept is based on the fact that most records become less useful over time. This enables us to look at the different stages of the record's 'life' much as we might look at the life of a biological creature (Government of the Northwest Territories, Canada, 2002).

- *Active (or current)* – the record is created or received and is frequently referenced and used by staff for its original purpose(s). Records are usually kept in offices or shared file systems while they are active.

- *Inactive (or semi-current)* – the record is no longer needed on a daily basis for business as usual but often must be retained for financial or legal reasons. Inactive records are frequently moved from offices to be stored in a records centre or off site, where they can be maintained and retrieved if needed at a low cost to the museum.

- *Final disposition (either destroy or transfer to archive)* – at this stage, the record is no longer needed for the purpose for which it was created. It should be destroyed or transferred to the archive where it will be permanently preserved for access over the long term.

Figure 2.1 The records life cycle

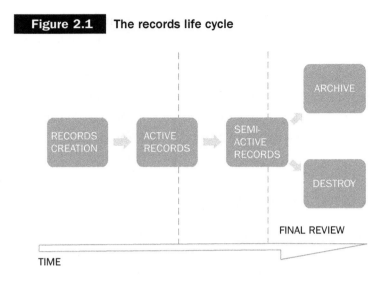

There are no formally established guidelines about exactly how much material should be destroyed and how much should be transferred to the archive. It depends on a number of factors, including the legislative requirements of the business and the nature of the business carried out by the organisation. In museums, the widely accepted figures are 85 per cent and 15 per cent. Specifically, roughly 85 per cent of records can usually be destroyed once the inactive period is over. The remaining 15 per cent or so (including record types such as accession or object files and condition reports) have archival value and should be transferred to a proper long-term storage environment (often on site for ready reference, but in some cases off site) where they can be retrieved for historical or research use by external researchers or museum staff under secure invigilation.

The 15 per cent figure is slightly higher than for conventional institutional archives. This is because in museums many records, such as accession files and exhibition records, remain 'permanently active': they support and facilitate the everyday business of managing historic assets over time, from when they are created until (and beyond) when the museum ceases to exist.

In other situations, for instance where the institutional archive of an organisation has been transferred to an external place of deposit (such as a county record office[6]) in which the records will be made available solely for research purposes, the figures for disposal and permanent retention are more likely to be in the region of 95 per cent and 5 per cent respectively.

The records continuum

The life-cycle concept makes a sharp distinction between current and archival record keeping. A newer Australian approach, called the *records continuum* (Figure 2.2), provides a slightly different way of thinking about the integration of records management and archival processes which is especially useful to museum records managers/archivists.

Figure 2.2　**The records continuum**

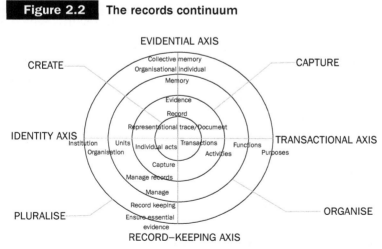

Source: Based on www.infotech.monash.edu.au/assets/images/research/
groups/rcrg/publications/continuum-diag.gif, by kind permission of Frank Upward.

The continuum approach accepts that record-keeping practices carry records forward for multiple purposes by many people over time (Pearce-Moses, 2005). This approach means that the archival record is still essentially active. Some museum records series, such as accession files, object documentation, exhibit files and conservation records, benefit from this approach, as they have simultaneous multiple values or life stages, as 'permanently active' records that possess both evidential and historical value over time. The concept allows us to see records keepers as contributors to an ongoing intellectual process applied to the records within the organisation. This is why policy and procedures state that everyone in an organisation is a records manager to some degree and must take responsibility for the health of the records they create, use, share and hold.

Records series

The record series is an important concept in records management because it is the level at which records should be managed. A *record series* is a group of related records which are often used and filed as a unit and may have been produced as a result of the same activity. The idea is that a document, for instance a letter, lives within a file that belongs within a series. Most decisions about how to manage the document are made at the series, rather than at the document, level.

Examples of series created by most museums include:

- annual reports
- press cuttings
- recruitment files
- correspondence relating to enquiries
- board of directors' meeting minutes

- accession registers
- event booking forms
- curatorial research correspondence.[7]

It is much easier to deal with the huge quantity of records created, held and used if they are managed as record series. Making decisions about arranging, storing, retaining or disposing of them at the individual item level is simply too time consuming. Instead, it is better to rely on the context of the record to manage it and ensure that, when it needs to be accessed, it can be fully understood. Managing records at series level does not necessarily involve imposing a new order on existing records. Record creators usually keep records in series even if they are not labelled or consciously treated as such. This natural order of arrangement may simply need to be teased out. Records management involves identifying record series and putting in place measures to ensure that these groups of records are managed systematically.

The definitions, concepts and ideas discussed in this chapter form the basic principles of records management that apply to all organisations, including museums. It is important to understand them in order to communicate and apply them within the museum context. The next chapter addresses how to present a business case for implementing museum records management.

Notes

1. Remember that *records* document transactions and decisions. Non-records are *ephemeral* materials that can include routine e-mails, copies of minutes and other policy documents and drafts.
2. See *www.collectionslink.org.uk/RMRecords* (accessed: 31 March 2010).

3. See *www.ucl.ac.uk/~uczcw09/appraisl/characs.html* (accessed: 26 March 2010).

4. The entire body of records of an organisation, family or individual that have been created and accumulated as the result of an organic process reflecting the functions of the creator (Pearce-Moses, 2005).

5. The UK convention uses 'archive' in the singular; the American in the plural (archives), unless referring to a set of materials created by the same person or group of persons or organisation, where the records of multiple organisations are held in one institution.

6. Transfer in this instance is not the same as simply using off-site storage for inactive records or archives.

7. See *www.museuminfo-records.org.uk/resources/RMe%2D tool/* (accessed: 31 March 2010).

3

Making a business case for records management

Sarah R. Demb

Abstract: Explores how to compile a business case for records management, including how to calculate the cost of records and manage risk. Discusses the importance of communicating records management to staff across the museum.

Key words: business case, communication, cost-benefit analysis, quick wins, risk assessment.

Introduction

The role of a records manager can be challenging, particularly if records management is a new focus within the museum. Even if there is a clear need to improve record keeping, it is not unusual to face initial reluctance from colleagues. It is common to encounter the following arguments.

- The institution has managed perfectly well without records management. Why now?
- There is no time to introduce records management – staff are overstretched already.
- How will records management save the organisation money?
- It is just paper/data: why does it matter?

It is important to address these concerns. Records management is not an isolated activity. On the contrary, since every computer user is a record creator of some type, a successful records management programme is likely to involve staff across the organisation. Communicating its benefits at all levels is vital, and it is important to begin this process before implementing procedures or starting work with the records themselves.

In regard to communicating, one important element to take into account is the relationship the records manager has with the information technology (IT) department. It is unusual for the records manager to sit within the IT department, although as the volume of paper records decreases in proportion to those 'born digital', this might start to make more sense. Because all the records management principles and practices described in this book apply equally to paper and electronic records, it is imperative to have a collaborative approach with the IT team. This significant relationship will be crucial when establishing policy regarding the contemporary file plan, as outlined in Chapter 7 (an authorised structure involving the museum network, shared drives and PCs), implementing file-naming conventions, capturing e-mail as records, agreeing which metadata are needed and how they will be kept about files, and applying records retention schedules to electronic records (such as those kept in database systems or intranets).

The IT team not only helps to implement records management policy, but is responsible for ensuring that records management functionality is applied to any corporate proprietary systems brought into the museum. The records manager will need to flag that functionality to the IT team and work closely with the team to integrate it into systems. Greater and earlier intervention by records managers with records creators and IT teams is necessary within the electronic records environment. The business case described below relies on close liaison with IT for a thorough knowledge of the way records management will benefit its functions.

This chapter explores how to compile a business case for senior management and secure a mandate, as well as the importance of communicating records management practices to colleagues.

Compile a business case

Step 1: Understand the institutional context

Before compiling a business case, it is vital to understand the particular record-keeping situation in the institution. Spend a few weeks fact-finding and putting records management into context. It is important to have clear and ready answers to the following questions.

- What are the current records management issues?

- What are the (key) risks of not implementing records management?

- What is/will be the records manager's role in the organisation?

- How will records management benefit the institution?

- What resources are needed to achieve records management goals?

- What is the implementation plan?

Consider the situation beyond a records management perspective; take into account the views of staff – and particularly those of senior managers, as they may not always be the same. It is not necessary to scope a full action/implementation plan at this stage, but it is important to identify specific solutions and practices that would be appropriate to, and welcomed by, the institution. Anticipate how systematic records management will impact on the organisation.

Step 2: Assess risk

Risk management is a systematic process of identifying, analysing and responding to risk across all functions in an organisation (JISC, undated). It is a strategic approach that *anticipates problems* and attempts to prevent or mitigate them; by managing records well, the museum is in effect managing risk. It is common for many museums to have at least one master risk register that describes and rates risks, and outlines the ways to mitigate them. Use the museum's risk register template to outline the information and records management risks; that is, the current risks that could be mitigated by implementing a records management programme.

Examination of the museum's risk register(s) is likely to show that many of the risks already catalogued are informational in nature and can be mitigated by effective records management.

Risk evaluation should include an examination of the museum's compliance with relevant legislation (as this is a substantial subject, it is examined in more detail in the next chapter).

To conduct a risk assessment, you must establish your risk criteria, decide what might be at risk and how/why, identify any current controls, calculate a risk rating based on likelihood (probability) and severity of impact (consequences) and then decide what (records management) steps must be taken to eliminate or control the risk. Figure 3.1 shows a sample assessment[1] of two organisational risks.

A *full risk assessment template* is given in Appendix 1, including sample risk criteria and a scoring framework.

| Figure 3.1 | Risk assessment template |

The risk Numbered list of what can happen The source Bullet points of how it can occur	Current controls and their effectiveness E = Effective P = Partially effective I = Ineffective	Actual risk rating Likelihood a. Almost certain b. Likely c. Possible d. Unlikely e. Rare x Impact 5. Insignificant 4. Minor 3. Moderate 2. Major 1. Severe = Risk level F. Negligible E. Low D. Medium C. High B. Extreme A. Severe	Treatments What steps do we take to mitigate this risk further?	Residual risk rating (after treatment) Likelihood x Impact = Risk level	Treatment completion date and/or Date of next review	Risk owner (Name and job title)
1. Lack of comprehensive oversight and control of held information · Lack of understanding regarding data privacy issues	Training on museum records management (P) Data protection policy and procedures implemented (P)	a x 2 = C (High)	Review compliance with specific legislation (e.g. Data Protection Act) Roll out training as part of mandatory induction and provide refresher training on demand or as needed	c x 4 = E (Low)	June 2012	Records manager
2. Failure to recover well from a major incident · IT records cannot be recovered · No centralised records management programme in place	Disaster recovery plan in place (P) Emergency planning in place (P) Reliable external back-up of all data (P)	d x 2 = D (Medium)	Review of IT system and security Records management policy and procedures in place	d x 3 = E (Low)	June 2012	IT with records manager

Step 3: Calculate cost savings and describe the value of records

Keeping records as evidence, whether for operational or legal reasons, already costs the museum staff time and storage space (both physical and virtual). The best way of reducing these costs is to manage records in a systematic and proactive way. At the same time, records identified as having administrative, legal, evidential or research value are worth keeping properly. Any money the museum spends on managing records should be spent on these records.

By managing risk as above, the museum will mitigate costs and maximise the value of its records. Using records to manage risk actually increases their value to the museum and ultimately reduces its overall costs. This means that any investment the museum makes in implementing records management – whether in staff time, storage space or supplies – pays dividends by protecting the museum against litigation, enhancing its reputation for information management and services and helping staff to operate more effectively. After the initial investment, the costs should decrease rather than increase.

The museum already spends money on records management, even if it is unacknowledged. Records storage (whether office space, shared drives or other designated space), retrieval (staff time spent looking for records) and information systems (such as databases) all cost the museum money every day.

Identify the museum's most costly information and records management spend

There may be a tendency to look to technological solutions, such as archiving systems which have the capacity to store 'everything', and that demand large amounts of consultant and staff time to make them usable and train colleagues to use them. It is probable that by managing records correctly the museum may achieve less or no spend on these systems. One of the keys to decreasing monetary costs is to address whether the museum needs to store all the information it currently holds. Once it is possible to determine what needs to be kept, and for how long, consider what resources are required to do so.

For instance, not all e-mail must be kept in the medium or long term if proper records schedules are in place to weed ephemeral and other unneeded communications, thus creating savings on museum server space. Museums that outsource e-mail services can thus realise immediate savings by applying retention schedules. As discussed earlier, the museum archive should permanently store only about 15 per cent of all the records the organisation creates. This figure can be used to calculate paper and electronic records storage costs.

Tip

To do a cost-benefit analysis, ask these key questions.

- Are any records stored unnecessarily?
- Are there ways to save on server space by deleting non-records information identified in the records survey?
- Does the museum need to host systems externally or is it more affordable to bring this in-house (or vice versa)?
- Is the museum paying for off-site storage of inactive paper records that can be disposed of? These running costs can often be reduced.

Calculate possible savings

Calculate possible savings by determining how much the museum spends per square metre on office space or per gigabyte in server space (if the museum rents its premises or outsources its servers, this information should be readily available; if the museum owns its home and servers, the calculation can be based on rates and other building maintenance costs, and on the money spent annually by IT to increase digital storage). Then determine the average amount of office or server space used by each staff member, including records storage. If colleagues are using office or server space to store inactive or duplicate records that can be destroyed or stored off site in cheaper accommodation, then applying records management practices will result in monetary as well as space savings.

For example, museums create certain types of new records every year to provide evidence of how they spend their budgets and document their object collections and exhibitions; so finance records, accession files, object records and exhibition files usually increase at a rapid (although possibly steady) rate. It is possible to calculate how much the museum spends on storage of these records every year.

Tip

Storage cost calculation.

Space^2 cost per square metre (based on rent rate for physical space): £45/m^2

Volume of new records created each year (finance records): 5 m^2

Cost: £45 x 5 = £225

If this cost is applied to paper finance records which need to be kept no longer than six years, then proper disposal of a backlog of those records at the right time will save the museum £225 per year of records and 25 m^2 of space.

If these records are series that need to be kept permanently, such as accession files or selected exhibition records, then the cost can be evaluated against the frequency of retrieval – is there a cheaper (non-office) storage site where the records can be kept? Or is the museum willing to spend that money on storing records to which staff need daily access?

Similarly, determine how much of the material on servers is duplicate information, how much is inactive and how much is taken up by multiple back-ups which are not needed. Determine how much the museum spends annually on server costs using historical data from IT and financial records – if the cost increases every year, the chances are there are savings to be made. It is true that information increases exponentially, but not all information needs to be kept; money should be spent strategically on records storage. For example, if staff need to request increasingly large amounts of server space for e-mail inbox storage, ensuring proper records management of those messages can bring costs down.

The main cost savings are usually in records storage space in offices and the increased efficiency of staff when retrieving records, but be aware that some costs are not monetary; for example, they may be reputational (e.g. negative publicity or legal sanctions related to the inability to locate information and records for FOIA requests).

Step 4: Identify the appropriate place to get a mandate

A general rule of thumb when seeking a mandate for records management is: the more senior, the better. Raising awareness high up in the institution will not only help to educate staff, but will also encourage them to carry out relevant records management activities. Ultimately, since all museums and galleries have legal imperatives for records management, it is important to ensure that those staff who would be liable in case of a breach are aware of the risks. It should be relatively easy to identify the senior decision-making bodies. These are likely to include:

- trustees or governors
- director
- curators
- other senior managers, including the post responsible for planning and implementing IT.

Successful records management is only achieved by gaining the active support of colleagues and it is important not to alienate anyone. If seeking a mandate involves consulting with a number of different bodies, then do so. Poor record keeping can be disastrous to an institution (and conversely good record keeping can have enormous benefits): it is the records manager's job to ensure that those in authority are aware of this. Support from senior staff will be critical to the success of the work.

Step 5: Present the business case for records management

Once a snapshot of the museum's record-keeping situation is established (including calculation of risks and costs), and it is clear where to secure authority, the final stage is to present a business case for records management. It should address the following questions.

- What are records? What is records management?
- Why is records management necessary for the institution (outline the risks and opportunities or benefits such as costs savings)?
- What is the proposed plan of action?
- What resources are needed to implement the programme (e.g. staff, facilities)?

- How does records management fit in with the museum's mission, vision, major projects or other initiatives?

Essentially, the business case should *broaden understanding of records management and clearly demonstrate how it will benefit the institution.* The value of this cannot be overestimated: securing a mandate before starting will not only help ensure the programme is successful, but will also reduce the overall workload. If staff cannot see the benefits of the records management programme and are not lured by the 'carrot', then mandate from a senior body is a useful 'stick'. A business case example is given in Appendix 2.

The importance of communication

Records management cannot happen in a vacuum. It depends on the input of the museum and its staff. To ensure success, it is important to *present the business case* for records management to all staff, not just those who hold the resources needed to implement a programme.

Many administrative or operational records do not directly concern the object collections, and historically have been considered of lesser importance to the museum. This means that while some records that relate to functions such as health and safety, human resources or finance may have been managed in a systematic way due to legal requirements, others may have been neglected. Getting staff to understand that these records also contain information valuable to the institution and are worth managing properly (not just to comply with the institution's legal requirements) may present a challenge.

Both the business case and internal communications about the programme should be promulgated with the following principles in mind.

Avoid jargon

While it is helpful to know the terms used by records management specialists, there is no need to use them if colleagues will be more comfortable with prosaic descriptions – whether specific to the museum sector or to certain generic functions like finance or human resources. A good communicator can creatively present records management using professional language and be prepared to explain terms.

For example, records management often refers to *records groups* and *records series* as a hierarchical way of conceptualising and organising records. They can also be explained by describing the museum's shared drive (the records group) and its component folders (records series).

In some instances it may even be best to avoid using the term 'records management' altogether, since it does not immediately suggest the benefits to individual staff. Using project or programme titles that focus on the end result may be the best way to gain support. It also encourages shared ownership of the work needed and helps remove the idea that the goals have been generated solely by the records manager or team. Common terms communicate museum-wide ideas.

For example, an initiative to rationalise and better organise shared drives might mean more to people if it is called a 'Sharing information' project. Efforts to review records housed in a neglected storage area might best be communicated by being referred to as 'Maximising space' or a 'Records tidy-up'. *Strike a balance between terms that communicate a systematic approach and those that are meaningful to staff in the museum's context.* Records management terms can convey the authority needed to carry out the work.

Know the audience

Aim explanations at the right level. Senior management will want and need a different explanation to operational staff carrying out the actual work. In a small museum one message may be suitable for everyone, but in a larger museum some staff – like administrators – may want to know more about the 'how' than the 'why' (although both are important to impart), especially if they are to become 'records champions'. It is also important to explain the bigger picture to staff in a meaningful way. Be as context-specific as possible. For example, 'faster access to records' may be better expressed as 'being able to find exhibition images easily on the shared drive'.

Do some 'quick wins'

Enabling some tangible benefits very early on will both win support and demonstrate what records management is all about. In the early days, these 'quick wins' often go further to show the benefits of a systematic approach than any memo or policy. Saying 'yes' to requests for help with tasks that staff may carry out themselves later on will foster goodwill and give people a better idea of what records management means.

Quick wins demonstrate the offer of a tangible service and staff will see the benefits of the work immediately. This will encourage them to understand the records management programme and the work they will need to contribute. Make a list of 'quick-win projects' for staff to consider.

Tip

Quick wins can include these activities.

- Normally you will probably need staff to list and pack up their own records before an office move or transition, but early on it may be judicious to make some exceptions and do it yourself – or help them with it – to demonstrate how much easier it makes it to find records.

- Walk a colleague through the process of deciding what e-mail can be deleted. You will not always be able to focus on this level of detail, but in the early days it might be useful to demonstrate that it can be easily accomplished.

- If there is space, consider temporarily storing records that could otherwise be disposed of immediately if a department is nervous about getting rid of them. You can review the situation and the records schedule at a later date.

- Work with a team or department to tidy up its part of the shared drive as a pilot, which can then be presented to the rest of the museum as a *fait accompli* and a path forward. This will also allow you to identify any issues that will arise and to workshop solutions.

- Review a discrete set of records in a particularly inaccessible storage area to demonstrate that this type of work can be done. Key records such as building plans are often stored in difficult spaces due to their awkward shapes and sizes; making them more accessible is a win-win situation.

Use appropriate forums

Identify how staff prefer to find out about new initiatives and determine the learning preferences of the museum. If some staff enjoy using interactive 'e-tools' on their own, explore offering this option.[3] Note the schedule for regular all-staff meetings which ensure that most people will learn about initiatives in a timely manner. Perhaps department meetings are the best forum in which to customise a message to specific museum functions. Consider offering one-to-one tutorials on a rolling basis for those who request them. If records management policies and procedures can be included in the museum's induction programme, then do this early on – it should certainly be a programme goal. Often, a combination of some of the above is most effective. Do not assume that everyone will understand records management the first time around – be cheerful and willing to explain more than once.

Fit records management into the larger context

Communicating what records management is will be much easier if it is integrated into any existing initiatives, projects or similar work. The point is to embed records management into normal workflows, both to show staff that it is not extra work and also to demonstrate that it can easily fit into how they already approach their tasks.

Do not underestimate the importance of talking enthusiastically to everyone about records management more than once. In a busy museum environment in which work is fast-paced and project-oriented, records keeping is often low on the list of priorities. Be upbeat and definite about the value of the work. The best advocates for records management are the staff who have experienced its benefits.

Tip

Embed records management across the museum.

- Include specific record-keeping responsibilities in staff contracts or job descriptions.

- Work on linking records management to related policies such as information security and IT guidance materials.

- Work to make data protection statements consistent across the museum on all relevant forms (such as visitor comment cards), your museum's website and in appropriate policies and procedures as per the examples in Appendix 6.

- Build records management into procurement processes, public programmes procedures and existing IT, exhibition and project handbooks.

Notes

1. This is based on the template developed and used by the Museum of London.
2. There is an inherent tension here, as paper records are usually measured in linear metres, but it is easy to measure square metres for this purpose.
3. See *www.museuminfo-records.org.uk/toolkits/Records Management.pdf* and *www.museuminfo-records.org.uk/toolkits/InformationPolicy.pdf* (accessed: 31 March 2010).

4

Legislation and records management requirements

Charlotte Brunskill

Abstract: Explores the most significant pieces of relevant legislation. Provides a summary of each Act, identifies sections of legislation particularly pertinent to record keeping, outlines penalties for non-compliance and explores practical implications of compliance.

Key words: legislation, compliance, Public Records Acts, Local Government Acts, data protection, freedom of information, environmental information, penalties.

Introduction

Legislation has had a profound impact on the practice of managing records – particularly public records – in the UK. Until the latter part of the last century, the majority of enactments focused on archive records. It was not until the 1990s that active and semi-active records were considered. There is no overarching UK code of archives or records legislation; instead, a number of measures govern record-keeping practices. This chapter explores the most significant pieces of this legislation. Along with providing a summary of each Act, it identifies sections of the legislation that are particularly pertinent to record keeping and, where relevant, outlines penalties for non-compliance and explores the practical implications of compliance. Acts are listed in chronological order.

Public Records Acts 1958 and 1967

The Public Records Acts (PRA) 1958 and 1967 form the main legislation governing public records in the United Kingdom.

A full definition of public records is given in the first schedule, section 10(1) of the PRA 1958. A more straightforward explanation provided by the National Archives (1999) is as follows:

> If the creator of a record was a central government department, agency or body, or predecessor to a modern department of state, funded from Treasury funds granted through parliamentary vote, then its records are likely to be public records falling within the definition and scope of the Act.

The Public Records Acts apply to scheduled national museums and galleries.[1] However, their provisions are of interest generally because they enshrine UK best practice in the management of archive records.

The PRAs established a cohesive regulatory framework covering public records in the UK. The 1958 Act instituted the principle that public records identified as being worthy of permanent preservation should be housed and made available to public inspection in a single repository: the Public Record Office (PRO).[2] The Act also stipulates that records would be transferred to the PRO 30 years after creation and that most would be opened 50 years after creation. The time of opening was subsequently reduced to 30 years by the PRA 1967. This has recently been reviewed (due in part to the exigencies of the Freedom of Information Act) and a phased reduction of the closure period (from 30 to 20 years) will begin in 2013.

Section 4 of the Act also makes provision for public records to be preserved in specially designated 'places of deposit' – organisations outside the PRO that afford suitable facilities for the safekeeping and preservation of their records. In addition to being the primary place of permanent deposit of the official record of government, the PRO – now called The National Archives (TNA) – is the central advisory body on the care of records and archives in the UK, and is charged with the practical business of ensuring that the provisions of the Acts are carried out. TNA is also responsible for setting standards, supporting innovation and promoting good practice in information and records management across the UK.

The PRAs are primarily concerned with the permanent preservation of records from an archival perspective, but are also relevant to records management, because in order to sustain a good archive over the long term, organisations must have effective record-keeping practices in place at the point that records are created.

Key sections

Key sections of the PRA 1958, with particular reference to record keeping, are as follows.

- §3(1) – Selection and preservation of public records. Public organisations have a duty to create, select and permanently preserve records which have long-term historical value.

- §5(5) – Access to public records. Public organisations have a duty to ensure that records preserved because they have long-term historical value are made available to the public.

Penalty for non-compliance

Under section 4(3) the Lord Chancellor (at the behest of TNA) can direct that records be returned from their place of deposit to TNA if the provisions of the PRA are not being carried out. Specifically, the records of selected organisations can be removed to the care of TNA (or another suitable place of deposit) if they are not managed appropriately.

This can be a very useful driver for implementing records management in the relevant national museums, since the nature of museum work means that some staff, including registrars, conservators and curators, need constant access to archival records (particularly object and accession files) in order to do their jobs. TNA is tasked with inspecting places of deposit to ensure that the appropriate standards are met. In practice, TNA is reluctant to remove public records from places of deposit, but prefers to work with the 'failing' organisations to ensure that improvements are made. The inspection process includes delivery of a report (usually to the director or highest authority in the museum) that highlights areas of concern. TNA inspection staff are happy to liaise with museum records managers to ensure this document is supportive of their work.

In 2004, as part of a remit to promote preservation of and access to archives of all kinds in the UK, TNA extended this inspection service. It developed a new 'Standard for Record Repositories'.[3] Although this document is primarily addressed to record bodies holding public records, specialist repositories and private owners (both individuals and organisations) are also encouraged to follow its provision. The introduction to the standard explicitly states that its recommendations are 'addressed to archivists and governing bodies of record offices, libraries, museums and other institutions holding records which are available to the public for research'. The provisions of the document are organised into five key areas: constitution and finance, staff, acquisition, storage and preservation. TNA works with any institution that wants to meet the standard. Essentially, its expertise on the management of records and archives is available to all types of museum.[4]

Practical implications for compliance

The TNA standard is detailed and must be read in full, but key issues for compliance can be summarised as follows. Organisations must:

- develop a policy statement establishing the objectives of the repository and the service it will provide (§1.3)

- employ sufficient staff to be 'commensurate with the extent and nature of records held and with the intensity of their use' (§2.4)

- develop a clearly defined statement of collecting policy identifying the subject areas, geographical scope and medium of material that will be collected by the institution, and ensure this policy is publicly available (§§3.2, 3.4)

- provide a designated study area for access and ensure that records open to inspection are clearly described and these descriptions are readily available (§§4.1, 4.7)

- ensure that records are stored broadly in compliance with the British Standard 5454 recommendations for the storage and exhibition of archival documents (§5.1.1).

Questions for records managers

If a museum is compliant with the PRA and the Standard for Record Repositories it will be able to answer 'yes' to both of the questions below.

- Is there a corporately approved method for identifying and securing records required for permanent preservation (i.e. retention decisions should not be based on space requirements or individual preference)?
- Are the records created by the museum in a fit state (easily retrievable, housed appropriately and protected securely) for public access?

Local government legislation

The Local Government (Records) Act 1962, the Local Government Act (LGA) 1972, the Local Government (Access to Information) Act 1985 and the LGA 2000 form the main legislation governing records of local authorities.

As discussed in Chapter 1, the LGAs listed above apply to museums operating under the aegis of the local authority. The record-keeping implications of the 1962 and 1972 Acts mainly concern archive records. In short, they provide for principal councils to preserve, provide access to and store their records in appropriate conditions. The Acts of 1985 and 2000 have implications for active and semi-active records.

Key sections

Key sections of the LGAs are as follows.

- LGA 1985, Part IIIA – Access to meetings and documents of local authorities, committees and subcommittees.
- LGA 2000, Part V – Miscellaneous, access to information, ss. 97 and 98.

Practical implications for compliance

The 1985 Act provides for the minutes, agendas, reports and background papers of meetings to be made available for public inspection. The 2000 Act requires local authorities to create and issue key strategic and decision-making documents (such as forward plans and the minutes of meetings). The legislation is primarily directed at core local authority operations, but may be applied to other organisations operating under local authority control. It is thus prudent for relevant museums to ensure they create good records of committee meetings and other decision-making bodies and that these are made available for public inspection. Regardless of legislation, society increasingly expects transparency from public organisations. Proactively providing access to key documents enhances reputation. It also supports compliance with the Freedom of Information Act (discussed later in this chapter), which applies to local authority museums.

Data Protection Act 1998

The Data Protection Act (DPA) 1998 is the main piece of legislation that governs the protection of personal data in the UK. It applies to data held on both computer and paper so long as, in the latter case, the data are held in a relevant manual filing system.[5] The DPA gives any individual the right to know what information an organisation holds about him/her, and sets out rules to make sure that this information is handled properly. The Act is regulated by the Information Commissioner's Office (ICO).

The Act applies to all organisations, whether public authorities or private companies, that process personal data – information that makes it possible to identify a living individual, including names, private addresses, dates of birth and contact details. All museums are subject to the DPA. Practical guidance detailing how the Act impacts on record keeping is surprisingly scarce. The code of practice[6] for archivists and records managers under section 51(4) of the Act (published 2007) is useful in this respect, however. Produced jointly by TNA, the Society of Archivists (now the ARA), the Records Management Society and the National Association for Information Management, and endorsed by the ICO, Chapter 3 focuses specifically on providing 'guidance for the processes that records managers carry out in the order in which they need to be addressed from the point of view of records managers'.[7]

Key sections

Key sections of the DPA, with particular reference to record keeping, are as follows. Principles listed in italics are those which have particular significance for record-keeping practices.

- Part III: Notification by data controllers. The data controller is required to provide the ICO with details about how it processes personal data. The ICO publishes certain details in the register of data controllers.[8]

- Schedule 1, Part I: The eight principles. In summary, these state that personal data shall be processed fairly and lawfully; obtained only for one or more specified and lawful purposes; adequate, relevant and not excessive; *accurate and, where necessary, kept up to date*; *not kept for longer than is necessary*; processed in accordance with the rights of data subjects under this Act; *held securely*; and not transferred to a country or territory outside the European Economic Area.[9]

- Schedule 1, Part II, 7(10): Right of access to personal data. The data controller has 40 calendar days upon receipt to reply to a *subject access request*.

Penalty for non-compliance

On 6 April 2010 the ICO's new power to issue monetary penalties came into force, allowing it to serve notices requiring organisations to pay up to £500,000 for serious breaches of the DPA. In practice, unless an institution is persistently and profoundly in breach, a financial penalty is unlikely. By far the bigger risk is reputational damage. Due to the nature of their work, museums are particularly sensitive to this issue, as stakeholders such as donors, patrons, owners and lenders of works are all vital to the success of daily business. If an instance of mismanaged personal information is exposed, this can have a disastrous effect on current and future business.

Practical implications for compliance – data protection survey

In order to comply with the provisions of the DPA, it is essential to *identify all instances where the museum collects and processes personal data*. It is impossible to adhere to the eight data protection principles if there is poor understanding of where, what and how personal data are being processed.

The absence of this information will also render the tasks of notifying the ICO, writing a data protection policy and managing subject access requests very difficult. For this reason, a key step in securing compliance with the Act is to *conduct a data protection survey*. Depending on the particular situation in the institution, it may be appropriate to carry out the data protection survey as part of a wider records survey (see Chapter 5) – for example, where records management is entirely new to the institution. Alternatively, conducting the data protection survey as a separate exercise might be preferable if, for example, data protection has been identified as an urgent issue.

Whichever approach is selected, it is important to remember that although the DPA undoubtedly has record-keeping implications, compliance should never be identified solely as a records management issue. The majority of the Act's provisions concern the collection and use (or 'handling') of data – specifically what happens when data are in the active stage of the life cycle – and for this reason, responsibility for compliance rests with staff across the museum. A data protection survey, since it involves colleagues, is a most useful means of raising awareness of this issue. While the records manager may be in charge of coordinating activities, staff should be responsible for compiling relevant survey information for their area of activity.

A data protection survey should identify:

- all record series containing personal data
- which post is responsible for each record series identified
- in what format the data exist
- where and how the personal data were collected (specifically, at the point of collection was a data protection statement visible?)

- how the personal data are being used (in the first instance, and any subsequent instances)

- whether the personal data are being shared with any third parties

- whether the personal data are being transferred outside the European Economic Area (this includes posting personal data on the internet).

The most effective means of collecting this information, bearing in mind the importance of involving staff, is usually via a survey questionnaire issued to all sections of the institution. The questions should concisely address the issues listed above, and must be written in straightforward language with any technical/legal jargon clearly explained. It is a good idea to design a questionnaire which must be completed for each series (i.e. one form per record series containing personal data, rather than one per section or department). This will help avoid confusion and ensure that the data returned are consistent. A sample data protection survey form can be found in Appendix 3.

Depending on the size of the museum, the questionnaire might be issued either to all staff (smaller institutions) or identified representatives – 'information champions' from each area of business (larger institutions). To ensure that the data returned are accurate and reliable it is a good idea to hold a pre-data-collection training session. The purpose should be to ensure staff are clear about exactly how to fill in the questionnaire. The following terms, in particular, will need to be explained: *personal data, data processing, relevant manual filing system* and *record series*.

It is important to issue a deadline for completion. When the questionnaires have been returned, the task of data compilation can begin. Ideally the results should be recorded electronically (in an Excel spreadsheet or simple Word document for example), so they can be consulted, manipulated and kept up to date with ease. Alongside identifying problem areas and issues to be addressed, the primary result of the survey should be to produce a list of all record series containing personal data created by the museum. Records produced by personnel and development activities are likely to feature heavily, but most museums create and manage a considerable amount of personal data outside these areas. The volume and range of records containing information about living individuals are often considerable. A list showing some of the record series containing personal data that are common in the museum sector can be found in Appendix 4.

Notification

The ICO maintains a public register of data controllers. Each register entry includes the name and address of the data controller, alongside details of all the types of personal information held and the ways in which it is processed. The register can be consulted online. Failure to notify is a criminal offence, and register entries must be renewed annually for a two-tier fee which depends on the size, turnover and nature of the organisation.[10]

Most organisations that process personal data must notify the ICO, but there are some exemptions. Of particular relevance for the museum sector is the exemption for 'not-for-profit' organisations; however, strict conditions apply. Full details can be found on the ICO's website,[11] but as a general rule the not-for-profit exemption normally applies to small organisations. There are also limits on both the type of data that can be processed and the processing that can take place. Even if an organisation is exempt, the ICO encourages voluntary notification.

Given the above, it is expedient for most museums to notify. If the data protection survey has been carried out satisfactorily the procedure should be straightforward. Of key importance is that the museum has a clear understanding of the personal data it holds and the different ways in which these are processed. It is important to remember that following initial notification, entries must be kept up to date. The museum must have a mechanism for identifying when it embarks on any new activities that will involve the processing of personal data. The records manager, owing to his/her knowledge of the museum's records, may be responsible for coordinating this activity across the institution. However, it is essential that staff across the museum are also involved in identifying new data-processing activities.

Data protection policy

The DPA does not state that organisations processing personal data must have a data protection policy in place. However, if an institution is found to be in breach of the Act, the existence of a coherent data protection policy will count very strongly in its favour. Indeed, if the organisation is serious about its responsibilities under the Act, a policy document that establishes how compliance will be achieved is essential.

A comprehensive policy should cover the following elements:

- summary of the Act
- scope of the policy
- definition of terms
- statement of principles

- responsibilities
- procedures, including reviews
- breach consequences
- date of policy approval.

As with all policies, it is important to ensure the document is approved at a suitably high level of authority. It is perhaps even more important to ensure that, following approval, its provisions are supported by training for relevant staff; everyone dealing with personal data must be aware of their responsibilities. Finally, the document should be subject to regular review, and adapted where necessary to reflect changes in business practice. Two sample data protection policies, which include assignment of staff responsibilities, are given in Appendix 5.

Data protection statements

The data protection survey should have identified all personal data collection activities carried out by the museum. It should also have highlighted any instances where this activity is carried out in the absence of a data protection statement.

Data protection statements facilitate compliance with the Act because they support the first data protection principle: that data must be processed fairly and lawfully. By notifying individuals of how their data will be used and giving them an opportunity to opt out, personal data can be said to have been processed in accordance with this principle. Essentially they secure consent for processing. There are two types of statement: opt out and opt in.

- *Opt-out statements* involve simply informing individuals of how their data will be processed. They do not require individuals to give explicit consent in order for processing to be carried out. Rather, submitting personal data on the form will be viewed as consent in itself. The onus is on individuals to contact the institution if they do not want their data used in the manner explained in the statement. Opt-out statements are generally used where data are processed in a manner which might be understood or reasonably predicted from the collection method.

- *Opt-in statements* involve informing individuals of how their data will be processed and asking them to give explicit consent for processing to be carried out. This is usually done via a 'tick-box' form. Opt-in statements are generally used where data are processed in a manner which might not be reasonably predicted from the collection method or where the data collected are *sensitive* (as defined by the Act).[12]

Data protection statements are very useful tools. Employed consistently and correctly, they remove uncertainty and reduce risk. If personal data have been managed in accordance with a data protection statement, it is very unlikely that processing will cause distress to data subjects. Should an objection arise, statements provide evidence of good practice. Remember also that in order to achieve these aims, the museum must maintain a record of consents so that it can determine who has agreed to each type of processing. This does not mean that every tick-box form needs to be retained. If the data are recorded electronically in a database, for example, it may be sufficient to flag details of consent within this. As long as the process is clearly documented and carefully managed, individual consent forms can be destroyed as scheduled. Also keep in mind that consents are not 'for life' and must be reviewed at regular intervals.

As this area of compliance is potentially complex, it is a good idea to seek legal advice when drafting and implementing statements. A selection of standard data protection statements useful to museums is given in Appendix 6; these provide a starting point, but must be adapted to fit the circumstances of the particular museum.

Procedures for responding to subject access requests

Part II of the Data Protection Act gives individuals right of access to personal information held about them. Under the terms of the Act, requests from individuals are known as 'data subject access requests'. They must be answered within 40 calendar days of receipt. In order to respond to requests effectively, organisations should have in place a *data subject access request form* that individuals can use to request personal data held about them (see Appendix 7 for a sample form), and a *data subject access request procedure* that informs staff how to identify and respond to requests.[13]

Records management benefits of compliance

If a museum is compliant with the DPA, it will be possible to:

- know what personal information it collects, creates and processes
- locate this information quickly
- keep personal data up to date
- destroy personal data when they are no longer needed so that they do not remain in filing cabinets or on computer systems indefinitely

- store personal information securely, whether in electronic or paper formats
- appropriately restrict access to personal data.

Freedom of Information Act 2000

The Freedom of Information Act 2000 introduces a public 'right to know' and gives any individual the right to request and obtain recorded information held by public authorities, unless there are good reasons to keep it confidential. The ICO is responsible for ensuring compliance. Public institutions have 20 working days from receipt to respond to a request.

The Act applies only to museums and galleries in the public sector. The Ministry of Justice should be contacted if there is uncertainty about whether or not the legislation applies.[14] The Act has many implications for public institutions, one of the most significant being that in order to answer a request for information within the allotted 20 days, a transparent record-keeping system is essential.

Key sections

Key sections of the legislation with regard to records management are as follows.

- Part 1, §10: Time for compliance with request – public institutions have 20 working days to respond to a request for information.
- Part 1, §19: Publication schemes – public authorities are obliged to provide information through a model publication scheme which should be made available on the institution's website.

- Lord Chancellor's Code of Practice on the Management of Records under §46.15 in particular:
  - Part I: 6.1(a) organisational arrangements – that there should be 'recognition of records management as a core corporate function'
  - Part I: 6.1(c) that lead responsibility for records management should be allocated 'to a designated member of staff at sufficiently senior level' and operational responsibility for records management should be allocated to a member of staff with the 'necessary knowledge and skills'
  - Part I: 7 policy – that 'authorities should have in place a records management policy... endorsed by senior management'.

Penalty for non-compliance

The ICO has the power to issue an enforcement notice – a legal order – to require a public authority to address its failure to comply with the FOIA. The notice explains what the public authority has failed to do and specifies what steps need to be taken in order to comply with the Act.

Failure to comply with an enforcement notice may result in the ICO referring the matter to the High Court, which can deal with the public authority as if it had committed contempt of court. Likewise, the public authority may appeal against an enforcement notice to the Information Tribunal.

In practice, most FOIA request responses are unlikely to reach this stage. When a complaint is made against a public authority, the ICO investigates the facts behind the complaint and may then issue a decision notice. This represents the ICO's final view on whether or not the authority has complied with the Act. Decision notices (including those issued to museums and galleries) can be easily and quickly referenced on the ICO website.[16]

A review of the 'decision notice' database reveals that many institutions have reached this stage and so this, in itself, does not present much of an impetus for the introduction of records management. By far the bigger risk concerns reputational damage. A large proportion of FOIA requests received by museums and galleries are from journalists. If handled poorly, these can result in adverse publicity.

If a public authority is found not to conform to the Records Management Code of Practice, the ICO may issue a written practice recommendation under §47 of the Act. This specifies which parts of the code have not been met and what the institution must do to remedy this. The ICO will continue to monitor the situation until it is satisfied that the authority is in full compliance. Failing to comply with the code of practice may mean that an institution is also failing to comply with the Public Records Acts, so in this case the sanctions detailed in the section on the PRAs above may also apply.

Practical implications for compliance

Publication scheme

Under Part I, §19 of the Act, museums must produce a guide to the specific information they hold and ensure that it can be easily identified and accessed by the general public. The most common means of ensuring availability is by posting a publication scheme on the internet. Information guides and their contents must be reviewed and updated on a regular basis.

Further advice – including a 'definition document' listing sector-specific guidance on the types of information the ICO expects museums to publish and list in their guides to information – is available on the ICO website.[17]

Requests for information: procedure

Under Part I, §10 of the Act, public institutions have 20 working days to respond to a request. Requests need to be recorded in writing (this includes e-mail), but do not need to specify the FOIA. The 'clock starts ticking' as soon as a request has been received. In order to answer requests effectively, museums should ensure that all staff can identify a request for information and understand the response procedure.

Museums are *information businesses* and so are well versed in answering enquiries and supplying information. In particular, curatorial staff are likely to receive and respond to many requests. In larger institutions, activities may be filtered through a central information or enquiries desk which traditionally answers queries on a huge range of subjects and every aspect of how the institution works. Prior to the FOIA, many organisations already operated under a maximum response time for enquiries which may have been less than the 20 working days allotted by the Act. The FOIA should not change existing efficiencies in this area. Indeed, it is important to distinguish between FOIA requests and routine business and correspondence. Museums will continue to receive significant volumes of enquiries.

Requests that do not ask for detailed held information, but instead ask questions such as 'can you tell me when x exhibition will open?' or 'when was x acquired for the collection?' can be treated as normal correspondence. Written requests for information that is routinely supplied – for example, public floor plans, an acquisition policy or an exhibition programme – can be treated as business as usual (as long as they are answered within the FOIA timeframe or published as part of the museum's publication scheme). Museums should decide whether they wish to record such enquiries; most already have a means to do so.

Advice from the ICO suggests that as a 'rule of thumb':

- if any information is held and needs to be actively considered, then the request should be treated as a formal request for information

- if it seems likely that the request for information cannot be disclosed, it should be formally recorded as a request for information. (Information Commissioner's Office, undated.a: 6.)

It is prudent for museums to develop an FOIA enquiries procedure to deal with requests falling into the above categories. The policy should cover key issues such as:

- how to log a request
- who is responsible for answering requests
- how to apply exemptions
- how and when to charge for requests.[18]

Consideration should also be given to how long FOIA request paperwork is maintained. Recommendations compiled by TNA suggest that material relating to individual FOIA requests should be retained for a minimum of three years after the close of the case, and that any paperwork (individual requests as well as policy and procedural records) which has led to the *development of best practice* should be kept permanently.[19] The ICO also recommends that where possible information regularly requested should become part of or integrated into the publication scheme.

Compliance with the Lord Chancellor's Code of Practice

The code of practice under §46 provides guidance to public authorities about the desirable practice for them to follow in order to discharge their functions under the FOIA. It establishes *records management* as an essential requirement for public institutions. The entire code is concerned with how this can be achieved, and is therefore relevant to anyone working in a records management role within a public museum. It is easy to read and, although only a supplement to the provisions of the Act (and not a substitute for the legislation), presents a series of important questions for public authorities. These include the following.

- Is records management a recognised activity within your institution (s. 6.1a)?

- Is records management a designated responsibility and is this responsibility assigned to an appropriately senior member of staff (s. 6.1c)?

Records management policy

Within the context of the code, these questions support the establishment of records management as a core function for public museums. Another important question raised by the code is 'Does your institution have a records management policy in place?' (s. 7).

According to the code, the policy should provide 'a mandate for the records and information management function and a framework for supporting standards, procedures and guidance'.[20] Although it states that the precise contents will vary depending on the nature and business of an organisation, it contains some relatively detailed advice about content. Specifically, the policy should:

- outline the role of records management in the institution
- identify and make connections to related policies within the organisation
- define roles and responsibilities across the organisation
- indicate how compliance will be monitored.

The policy should establish what records management means within the context of the museum environment. As discussed in Chapter 1, museums create, receive, acquire and maintain many kinds of records which might historically have been assigned different status and subject to very different management. The records management policy should clearly state that records management *encompasses all records* created by the museum in the course of its business, including records related to the object collections. One caveat, as mentioned earlier, is that if the museum maintains archive collections acquired from external sources (sometimes also known as collected archives or special collections), the policy might note that, although the FOIA covers these records, they do not fall under the records management policy.[21] A good place to address these issues within the policy is under section headings entitled 'scope' or 'definitions'.

Additional policy sections may include the following:

- legal basis for records management
- statement of principles
- staff responsibilities at each level
- procedures (reference to)
- breach and consequences
- policy review period.

Like all policies, it is important to ensure the document is approved by a senior authority. This is supported by s. 7.1 of the code, which states that the policy must be 'endorsed by senior management'. It is perhaps even more important to ensure that, following approval, its provisions are supported by training for relevant staff; everyone dealing with records should be aware of their responsibilities. The document should be subject to regular review, and adapted when necessary to reflect changes in business practice. Finally, s. 7.4 states that the authority should consider publishing the policy: most institutions achieve compliance by making the document available on the internet via their FOIA publication scheme webpages. In summary, the *records management policy* is an important document because it establishes records management as a corporate function. It should form a core part of any records management programme regardless of whether the FOIA applies. An example policy can be found in Appendix 8.[22]

Environmental Information Regulations 2004

The Environmental Information Regulations (EIR) 2004 give any individual the right to request and obtain information about the environment held by public authorities, unless there are good reasons to keep it confidential.

Environmental information includes information about the following.

- The state of environmental elements such as air, water, soil, land and landscapes, natural sites, coastal and marine areas, and biological diversity and its components (including genetically modified organisms).
- Factors including substances, energy, noise, radiation or waste (including radioactive waste, emissions, discharges

and other releases) affecting or likely to affect the elements of the environment.

■ Measures (including administrative measures) such as policies, legislation, plans, programmes, environmental agreements and activities affecting or likely to affect the elements and factors referred to above.

■ Reports on the organisation's implementation of environmental legislation.

■ Cost-benefit and other economic analyses and assumptions used in the framework of the above.

■ The state of human health and safety, including contamination of the food chain, conditions of human life, cultural sites and built structures inasmuch as they are or may be affected by the state of the elements of the environment referred to above.

The EIR apply only to museums and galleries in the public sector. The Ministry of Justice should be contacted if there is uncertainty about whether or not the legislation applies.[23] It is important to remember that while the regulations were written with public authorities such as local councils in mind, museums and galleries often hold many of the types of information detailed above. Consider carefully where this information may be held in your organisation and how it can be made accessible.

Key sections

Key sections of the legislation with regard to record keeping are as follows.

■ Regulation 4 – Organisations must:
  – progressively make environmental information available to the public

- take reasonable steps to organise their environmental information to make it easier to access and publish

- publish this information on the internet, where possible.

■ Regulation 5[2] – Public institutions have 20 working days (from the day after the request is received) to respond to a request for information.

■ Article 7(2) of European Directive 2003/4/EC – Sets out the minimum criteria on what public authorities are expected to disseminate proactively. This includes the following types of environmental information:

- policies, plans and programmes

- progress reports

- summaries of monitoring of activities

- environmental impact studies.

Worst-case scenario

The enforcement provisions of the Environmental Information Regulations are taken directly from the Freedom of Information Act 2000 (see above).

Practical issues for compliance

Identification of environmental information

In order to comply with the EIR, it is essential to identify all the environmental information created and managed by the museum. A key step in securing compliance with the regulations is to conduct an environmental information survey. Again, depending on the particular situation in the organisation, it may be prudent to carry out this work as part of a wider records management survey. The process for this is usually far simpler than for the data protection survey discussed above. A basic survey form containing a comprehensive list of all environmental information (as defined by the regulations) should be circulated across the museum and staff asked to identify any records they have falling into the categories. At first glance the list might appear remote, but it is surprising how many records are covered by the regulations. A sample list of record series containing environmental information common in the museum sector can be found in Appendix 9.

Making environmental information available

Organisations must make available all information which falls under Article 7(2). The regulations say that this should 'be progressively made available'. This means it should be actively published and updated. Information produced after 1 January 2005 must be made available electronically. Museums subject to the FOIA are required to maintain a publication scheme (see above). For these institutions, environmental information should be presented in the guide to information. Indeed, guidance from the ICO states that the publication scheme should include at least the minimum environmental information required by the EIR (Information Commissioner's Office, undated.b). Museums not covered by the FOIA are still required to publish environmental information proactively. It is not necessary for them to adopt a publication scheme, but information must be made available in a systematic way. If a museum is compliant with the EIR, it will be able to create and manage environmental information, proactively disseminate this and keep the information current.

> **Tip**
>
> Given the nature of environmental information, it is often found in records of work done under contract to the authority/museum. Museums should avoid agreeing confidentiality clauses which might conflict with FOIA or EIR requirements. *Contracts signed before the EIR and FOIA came into effect should be reviewed with all relevant parties bearing this in mind.* Later contracts usually contain boilerplate clauses which state that confidentiality clauses will not prevent the authority from releasing information under its other legal obligations.

Other relevant legislation

There are many other pieces of legislation that affect museums and necessitate a records management programme. It is not possible to provide an exhaustive list, since Acts are repealed and introduced on a regular basis. In addition, museums carry out specialised functions for which particular legislation may apply. It is important to determine the precise legal framework of the institution. What follows is a brief summary of some of the most significant legislation: the Acts listed below, although not primarily concerned with record keeping, have implications for most organisations in the museums sector with regard to the creation and retention of records. Although records managers should have a general awareness of the provisions of these Acts, a detailed understanding is not normally required, since staff working in the relevant area are likely to have the requisite expertise. For example, staff working in finance should have knowledge of the record-keeping requirements imposed by financial laws and regulations. Finally, since the legislation listed is not specific to the museum environment, but applies to an enormous range of different organisations and detailed guidance is readily available elsewhere, only a brief summary of the key points is provided below.

The *Health and Safety at Work Act 1974* is the main legislation underpinning health and safety in the UK. Its provisions are implemented via a series of regulations.[24] Essentially, there are three main reasons to maintain health and safety records:

- to ensure the employer is well placed to protect the safety of staff and the public

- to fulfil statutory regulations or as a prerequisite for carrying out particular activities

- to protect the employer in the case of litigation.

The records manager (working with the health and safety officer) will need to ensure that certain documents are created and others are maintained for the required amount of time in order to minimise risk. For some records, this may be a significant amount of time (for example, records pertaining to asbestos abatement should be retained for 40 years). Precise record-keeping requirements will vary depending on the business undertaken by the organisation. Although museums are not generally high-risk health and safety institutions, activities such as conservation, framing, art/object handling, exhibition building and fieldwork or scientific research may require consideration. It is likely that most organisations will be required to maintain some form of the following.

- Statutory records such as fire safety checks, register of dangerous substances (under the Control of Substances Hazardous to Health Regulations 1994), risk assessments, inspection of machinery and equipment, notification forms for accidents, fire certificates.

- Procedural records such as health and safety policy, safety procedures and manuals, training records, safety inspections.

The *Limitation Act 1980* establishes timescales within which action may be taken for breaches of law. For example, it provides that breaches of ordinary contract are actionable for six years after the event, whereas breaches of deed are actionable for 12 years after the event. These timescales have a direct impact on record keeping: in order to provide evidence in the event of a claim, organisations need to retain relevant records for the length of time a breach is actionable. The Act does not establish mandatory retention periods; rather it *promotes risk assessment processes* – organisations must weigh up the risk of receiving a claim after records have been destroyed against the cost of preserving the records and the potential cost of any claim that might be upheld. In the course of everyday business, museums and galleries enter into many simple contracts, including with educational freelancers and print suppliers, and lending and borrowing works for exhibition and display purposes. For this reason, the six-year retention period is applied to many records created by the sector. In some cases records can be destroyed immediately after this. In others they may be weeded significantly and only records having long-term value for research purposes retained. Examples are as follows.

- *Exhibition case files* – retain in their entirety for six years from close of exhibition, then review for archival value.

- *Development events file* – retain in their entirety for six years after event, then destroy.

- *Loans out files* – retain in their entirety for six years after work is returned to museum, then review for archival value.

- *Individual membership records* – retain in their entirety for six years after membership expires/ceases, then destroy.

There are many statutes which have implications for the retention of financial records, including the *Financial Services Act 1986*, the *Value Added Tax Act 1994*, the *Civil Evidence Act 1995* and the *Companies Act 2006*. The provisions of these Acts are complex, but a common element is that they introduce a standard six-year retention period for many financial records, which include journals, ledgers, invoices, gift aid forms and employee salary histories. Records managers should work with finance staff to establish appropriate record-keeping practices.

The *Companies Act 2006* forms the primary source of UK company law. It applies to any museum established as a business entity, and has various implications for record keeping. It places a statutory requirement on companies to keep certain records, and in many instances determines how long they should be maintained. The provisions of the Act are complex and must be read in full. Records managers should work with company secretaries or high-level administrators to ensure record-keeping requirements are met. However, the provisions for registers and minutes (and paperwork) of board and senior management meetings are likely to be of relevance to most organisations. For example, the Act requires that the following records are created and maintained – for the most part – for the life of the company:

- register of directors
- certificate of incorporation
- memorandum and articles of association

- board minutes (signed)
- written resolutions of the board.

There is no doubt that legislation has a significant impact on record-keeping practices: relevant enactments establish a statutory requirement to maintain certain records and can also determine retention periods. It is important to establish the precise legal environment of the museum and work with staff to develop appropriate record-keeping practices. Ultimately, implementing a records management programme which is sensitive to, and establishes retention periods for records based on, relevant legislation will help ensure the museum is not vulnerable to sanctions or loss of reputation due to breaches.

Notes

1. The Public Records Act 1958, First Schedule, Part II, Other Establishments and Organisations, includes a full list of museums covered.
2. In 2003 the Public Record Office merged with the Historical Manuscripts Commission to become The National Archives.
3. See *www.nationalarchives.gov.uk/documents/standard2005.pdf* (accessed: 20 April 2010).
4. See also *www.nationalarchives.gov.uk/information-management/ our-services/services-to-archives.htm* (accessed: 20 April 2010).
5. According to the ICO, relevant manual filing systems mean non-automated records that are structured in a way which allows ready access to information about individuals – for example, correspondence arranged A–Z by sender.
6. See *www.nationalarchives.gov.uk/documents/dp-code-of-practice.pdf* (accessed: 20 April 2010).
7. Code of practice for archivists and records managers under section 51(4) of the Data Protection Act 1998, section 1.6.

8. See *www.ico.gov.uk/ESDWebPages/search.asp* (accessed: 20 April 2010).

9. The eighth data protection principle states that 'Personal data shall not be transferred to a country or territory outside the EEA unless that country or territory ensures an adequate level of protection for the rights and freedoms of data subjects in relation to the processing of personal data.' A full list of countries in the EEA and a list of countries providing adequate protection can be found on the ICO website at *www.ico.gov. uk/for_organisations/data_protection/the_guide/principle_8. aspx* (accessed: 20 April 2010).

10. See *www.ico.gov.uk/for_organisations/data_protection/notification/cost.aspx* (accessed: 11 December 2010).

11. See *www.ico.gov.uk/upload/documents/library/data_protection/ practical_application/gpn_not_for_profit_v1.0_web_version.pdf* (accessed: 20 April 2010).

12. Under the terms of the Act, 'sensitive includes personal data concerning racial or ethnic origin; political opinions; religious beliefs or other beliefs of a similar nature; trade union membership; physical or mental health or condition; sexual life; commission or alleged commission of any offence, or proceedings for any offence committed or alleged to have been committed'.

13. Further information and guidance about these requirements are available on the ICO website at *www.ico.gov.uk/for_ organisations/data_protection/the_guide/principle_6/access_ to_personal_data.aspx* (accessed: 20 April 2010).

14. See *www.justice.gov.uk/about/freedom-of-information.htm* (accessed: 20 April 2010).

15. The code is available at *www.justice.gov.uk/guidance/docs/ foi-section-46-code-of-practice.pdf* (accessed: 20 April 2010).

16. See *www.ico.gov.uk/tools_and_resources/decision_notices.aspx* (accessed: 20 April 2010).

17. See *www.ico.gov.uk/what_we_cover/freedom_of_information/ publication _schemes.aspx* (accessed: 20 April 2010).

18. Guidance on charging is available at *www.ico.gov.uk/for_ organisations/freedom_of_information/information_request/ costs.aspx* (accessed: 20 April 2010).

19. See *www.nationalarchives.gov.uk/documents/foi_sched_reten-tion.pdf* (accessed: 20 April 2010).

20. Lord Chancellor's Code of Practice, Section 7, Records Management Policy.

21. Further guidance on assessing whether deposited private archive collections are covered by the FOIA is available from TNA at *www.nationalarchives.gov.uk/documents/guidance_private_archives.pdf* (accessed: 20 April 2010).

22. Other examples are easily found online, as most institutions provide access to their records management policies on their websites.

23. See *www.justice.gov.uk/about/freedom-of-information.htm* (accessed: 20 April 2010).

24. These include, for example, the Noise at Work Regulations 1989; Manual Handling Operations 1992; Health and Safety (Display Screen Equipment) 1992; Control of Substances Hazardous to Health Regulations 1994; and Reporting of Injuries, Diseases and Dangerous Occurrences Regulations 1995.

5

The records survey

Charlotte Brunskill

Abstract: Explores the reasons to conduct a records survey and the importance of planning. Examines different survey types and methodologies, and discusses how to make effective use of the data collected.

Key words: comprehensive survey, targeted survey, direct survey, devolved survey, planning, objectives, stakeholders, methodology, interviews, analysis, results, reporting.

Why conduct a survey?

Whatever the particular situation in the institution, it is normally necessary to conduct an audit or survey before starting the practical work of implementing a records management programme. An effective survey will help to identify the issues, establish how significant these are, define priorities and ultimately draw up an action plan. It can also help lobby for resources. In most cases, the aim of a record survey is to gain a view of the overall situation in the museum.

- What records are being created?
- By whom?
- How are they used?

- Are they shared? And if so, by which staff?
- How are they stored?
- Where are they stored?
- How long are they retained and why?

Most importantly, what are the goals of the institution and what record-keeping systems are needed in order to support and achieve those aims? Establishing a complete overview of the record-keeping situation across the whole organisation is a vital stage in securing control over the records themselves. The survey is the foundation upon which the records management programme will be built.

Pre-survey: the importance of planning

To ensure that the audit yields the information needed to advance records management in the institution, it is important first to define the following clearly.

- *Objectives* – what must the survey achieve? What information is needed for this purpose?
- *Scope* – what elements will the survey encompass (format, location, subject matter of records)?
- *Methodology* – how will the survey be carried out?

The volume of records created by museums and galleries today is enormous and an *ad hoc* records survey can easily become overwhelming. Planning ahead for the survey is essential – not only does this ensure the data collected are relevant and useful, but it will also help ensure the work is completed in a manageable timeframe.

Step 1: Determine objectives

Before beginning work, it is important to determine the survey objectives. Exploring the following will help.

Stakeholders

Who, in the institution, is likely to be interested in the results of the survey? What information would they find useful? Consider the following.

- Records manager – what records are being created, by whom, in what format, where are they stored, for how long?

- Archivist (museum records) – which records have long-term value? In what format are they created, where are they stored and for how long?

- Freedom of information and data protection officer – which records contain personal information? How are records containing personal data managed (collected, stored, made secure, made accessible, time period retained)?

- Information desk/visitor services – how easy is it for staff to identify relevant job-related information? What methods are there for sharing information? What duplication exists?

- IT department – what formats of electronic records (word-processed documents, e-mail, databases, spreadsheets, digital images, etc.) does the museum create and how are these managed over time?

- Facilities – what space (physical and virtual) is currently taken up by storing records? What is the cost of this?

- All colleagues – can staff members easily locate the records they need to do their jobs? If not, why not?

Legal environment and best practice

What is the legal environment surrounding the institution (to what legislation is the institution subject)? What do the Acts say and what is their implication for record keeping? How does the institution aim to ensure compliance? What best practice might the institution adhere to? Consider all the factors explored in Chapter 4.

Other records-related initiatives

Are there any other projects which impact on record keeping and might influence data collection and priorities? Examples include the following:

- planned office moves (whether on site or to off-site locations)
- network tidy-ups (often when new servers are about to be installed)
- information policy review
- impending financial or other audits.

Recognised problems

What record-keeping problems have already been identified in the institution? Why has records management become a concern? What was the records manager post established to resolve/achieve? Examples include the following:

- identify and address duplication of records
- reduce storage space (physical and virtual)
- ensure legal or regulatory compliance
- improve work efficiency (by ensuring staff can locate and identify records).

Having investigated the above, draw up a focused list of aims: what are the key objectives that the survey, and ultimately the resulting records management programme, must achieve?

Step 2: Determine the scope of the survey

The next stage is to determine the scope of the survey. Essentially there are two options: survey everything or survey a targeted area.

A *comprehensive survey* (Figure 5.1) normally encompasses all the records of the institution. This involves looking at records:

- in all formats
- relating to all subjects
- in all locations.

Depending on the size of the institution, this may present a daunting task. However, bear in mind that it is not necessary to

Figure 5.1 Comprehensive survey: pros and cons

Benefits	Drawbacks
Requires participation of staff across the museum (a good way to begin educating the institution)	Requires involvement of staff across the institution (which can be difficult to achieve where records management is entirely new)
Produces a more holistic picture of the state of record keeping	Time-consuming and may not be realistic if the institution is large or there is a short project deadline
Results likely to be more accurate and present a firmer foundation for a records management programme	Results take more time to establish, meaning 'quick wins' are less likely or fewer; staff may lose interest or become disillusioned with records management if momentum is lost

focus on individual pieces of paper or even on individual files (although in some cases this may be necessary). The aim should be to identify *record series* or broad categories of records.

A comprehensive survey is usually suitable in the following environment:

- when the institution is already committed to records management – it has been recognised as an essential business function and/or the records management role is permanent or long term
- when there are no urgent issues to resolve
- when a comprehensive picture is required or has been requested.

A *targeted survey* (Figure 5.2) focuses on an identified area or group of records, usually limited by one or more of the following elements:

- record format (electronic, paper, etc.)
- subject matter (collections records, exhibitions records, etc.)
- creating body (section/department)
- physical location (particular shared drive, office, building etc.).

A targeted survey is usually suitable in the following environment:

- when the institution needs to make a business case for records management – where it is yet to be recognised as an essential business function and/or the records management role is temporary
- when there are immediately urgent issues to resolve
- when 'quick wins' have been requested.

Figure 5.2 Targeted survey: pros and cons

Benefits	Drawbacks
Does not necessarily require staff participation across the institution (and thus may be easier to achieve where records management is entirely new)	Lack of staff participation across the museum (which means an opportunity to educate them about records management is lost and will need to be addressed when the programme is rolled out)
Completed more quickly, therefore more opportunity for 'quick wins'	Produces only a partial view, therefore conclusions and expectations may need to be adjusted as records management is rolled out
Easier to implement where there is low appetite for records management	Has a limited impact on the institution; it may be necessary to extend the survey (to additional areas, records, etc.) at a later date
Possible to focus on particular issues or record groups to address long-standing problem areas	Risk of missing out on identifying problem spots or major issues

Time constraints must also be considered. Think about what needs to be achieved and the total time available. The records survey should take about a quarter of this time. The remaining three-quarters should be used for implementing recommendations and establishing a records management programme.

Step 3: Determine the survey methodology

The next stage is to determine the survey methodology. Essentially there are two choices: a direct audit, where all the data are collected by the records manager; or a devolved audit, where others are enlisted to collect data on the records manager's behalf.

A *direct survey* (Figure 5.3) involves the following key stages.

- Familiarisation with the institution.
- Define objectives and scope.
- Collect key documentation: floor plans; file plans (where they exist), etc.
- Plan questions and identify interviewees.
- Establish data collection tool (spreadsheet, database, etc.).
- Draw up survey schedule identifying when and for how long visits to each area will take, etc.
- Identify and brief relevant staff across the institution.
- Interview relevant staff.
- View each room.
- View shared drives (including relevant 'my documents' areas).
- Enter data into spreadsheet or database.
- Write up department/section reports.
- Analyse data and report results and/or draw up action plan.

Figure 5.3 **Direct survey: pros and cons**

Benefits	Drawbacks
Process will ensure familiarity with record-keeping practices, making it easier to implement changes after the survey	Time-consuming (1–1.5 hours per interview) and labour-intensive (it is necessary to look at the physical and virtual storage spaces identified), and data will need to be written up after the visit
Data collection is direct and therefore potentially more reliable	Data collection process likely to be complex (need to become familiar with a large number of record series)
A unique opportunity to show staff their work is important to the museum and demonstrate that records management is part of what they already do	It is easy to run over time (and collect too much detail), particularly when encountering enthusiastic staff

Allow *at least* one day per ten staff members.

A direct survey is usually suitable in the following types of environment:

- small to medium-sized museums
- where stakeholders (staff to be interviewed) are easily identifiable
- where there are fewer time constraints or the project schedule is longer
- where there are no urgent issues to address.

A *devolved survey* (Figure 5.4) will involve the following key stages.

- Familiarisation with institution.
- Define objectives and scope.
- Establish network of local contacts.
- Plan questions and identify relevant stakeholders.
- Draw up survey schedule identifying when to issue questions, run workshops, etc.
- Issue questions to local contacts.

Figure 5.4 Devolved survey: pros and cons

Benefits	Drawbacks
Quicker to achieve	Less staff involvement in initial survey will mean more time is required after the survey to implement the records management programme
Process is less labour-intensive for records manager as record creators complete the survey	Results are potentially less complete and reliable as respondents may misinterpret questions or leave out some answers

- Run workshops or brief staff.
- Conduct 'mop-up' visits (where follow-up on survey results is required).
- Collect responses.
- Write up mop-up visit results.
- Analyse data.

Allow *at least* three to four weeks from issuing the survey for responses, but do not wait too long or questionnaires will fall to the bottom of the pile and not get returned.

A devolved survey is usually suitable in the following type of environment:

- large museums
- where there are strict time constraints
- where there are urgent issues to address.

Tip

Before beginning the survey, it is essential to have a broad understanding of museum operations and history. The following reading is often helpful:

- institutional histories
- organisational structure charts
- annual reports for the last two to five years
- business plans for the last three years
- employee telephone lists
- procedure manuals for major museum functions or activities.

Step 4: Identify preferred key terms

This may be the first time the museum has heard anything about records management, so think carefully about the terminology employed during the survey. Identify the terms that are most appropriate to the institution (those that are least likely to be misunderstood) and apply them consistently. Clearly define those terms that might cause confusion. These measures will ensure that the data returned by the survey are reliable. Key terms that need consideration include:

- information/records/data
- record group/record series/record collection
- vital records/important records/key records.

Step 5: Plan questions and identify stakeholders/interviewees

Having identified the objectives, scope, methodology and key terms of the survey, it is finally time to compile the questionnaire that will be used by the records manager (direct survey) or by staff (devolved survey) to collect the data. Whatever the breadth or scope of the survey, the questionnaire should be concise: ideally no more than 40 questions. The questions should be easily understood and not open to misinterpretation – where possible tick-box style answers should be employed. Most questions will be applicable to both electronic and paper records, although a few will be specific to format.

Remember that when interviewing, questions should be flexible enough to enable them to be asked at the appropriate level: overview questions to senior management; more specific questions to middle management/recordscreators/ administrators; and less complex questions to operational staff, or to those people who are responsible for/create fewer records.

The following information should always be included on the survey forms:

- contact details of person conducting the survey (where applicable)
- name of record creator (person/department/unit)
- title of records series/group
- summary/brief description of record series/group (for what purpose were the records created, what information do they contain?)
- records format (paper, electronic or hybrid)
- software environment (for example, Word document, Outlook e-mail, Access database, etc.)
- location of records (shared drive/file cabinet/room, etc.)
- storage method (e.g. locked cabinet, open shelves, network area, 'my documents', etc.)
- volume of records (in linear metres, cubic metres or kilobytes)
- data protection status (do records contain personal data?)
- EIR status (do they contain environmental information, as defined by the Act?)
- vital record status (is the record series essential to the successful running of the institution in case of disaster?)
- legal requirements (are the records required for legal purposes?)
- age (date range of records in years)
- status (is the information currently in use, how long is it needed, could it be destroyed or archived?).

Remember, there should be one form for each series. Sample survey questionnaires can be found in Appendix 10.

Identify interviewees

If the institution is medium to large in size, it is not practical to interview all staff or even to ask everyone to fill out a questionnaire (not least because the time taken to collate useful results would be enormous). However, it is important to collect data from a wide range of staff (senior management to operational personnel) and across the entire organisation so that all museum functions are represented.

Specific staff members should be always be included in interviews:

- heads of departments/divisions, and the director if possible
- executive assistants, personal assistants, department administrators
- one to two 'middle managers' from each department
- one or two administrative/operational employees in each department.

Some museum functions may have only one practitioner who creates records – do not miss them out. Also remember to include part-time staff and relevant contractors.

Step 6: Develop the data collection tool

Having established the questions, it is important to identify how the returned data will be stored. The ideal tool is one that enables easy analysis. The following applications are all suitable data collection tools:

- Excel or other spreadsheet forms
- Access or other databases
- online survey questionnaire and analysis tools (if these

are free, remember to ensure that the data are held securely and only accessible to authorised individuals; and also that they can be easily downloaded, manipulated and migrated for inclusion in post-survey reports).

Tip

Whatever application is selected, it should be planned and developed carefully. Make sure the process of entering or uploading the data will be straightforward and that, where necessary, automatic analysis of the data is set up as part of the system (see the data analysis section later in this chapter). Before starting the survey, test the data collection tool thoroughly with sample data.

Step 7: Schedule the work and communicate with staff

Since the survey is likely to involve interviews with colleagues, review of records and visits to records storage areas it will inevitably be disruptive. To minimise the potential upset it is important the work is planned carefully. If a direct survey methodology is being employed, appointments should be made in advance. Be clear about how much time will be spent in each area. Specify who will need to be involved, how long interviews/discussion will take and how much time will be spent looking at records independently. It will be particularly important to establish the procedure for review of electronic records. Will the survey encompass records in shared-drive areas only, or will it incorporate 'my documents' in personal drives? Is it necessary to look at the computer of each member of staff, or will a sample of selected employees be enough? Would asking staff about their e-records practices be sufficient?

If the devolved survey methodology is employed, it will be important to meet with the identified contacts in each area. Explain when the survey questionnaire will be sent out, when workshops or briefing sessions will be run and how long they have to conduct and complete the survey. Regardless of the method, the important thing is to draw up a project plan and communicate this to all relevant staff.

Tip

Pre-survey staff workshops or briefings should cover the following topics.

- What is a record?
- What is a record series/group?
- What to include in the survey (types and formats of records).
- How to measure volume of records (linear or cubic metres, kilobytes).
- How to respond to the questionnaire (show sample answers).

Step 8: Secure permission to survey

To ensure the survey is successful it must encompass, and therefore the records manager must secure permission to access, all records across the institution regardless of their format or content. This should include, in particular, confidential or sensitive records, and records stored on shared drives and in 'my documents' areas. If the direct survey methodology is employed this is imperative. If the devolved survey methodology is chosen it may be less relevant, but securing permission is nevertheless important because the returned survey results may need to be clarified or verified by consulting the records directly; and the process of securing permission to access all records emphasises and reinforces the scope of the survey and the records manager's authority to do the work.

Step 9: Demonstrate management support

Finally, once the survey has been carefully planned, it is important to confirm and demonstrate management support for the work. Even the best-planned and well-conducted survey will require staff time, and for this reason some people may be resistant. Without the full support of management, the survey will founder. Before the survey begins a senior member of staff (preferably the head of the institution or each departmental/divisional head) should send a message to all staff announcing the plan, explaining the importance of cooperation and establishing authority for the survey staff to view confidential or sensitive files. This message will provide the passport to all areas of the organisation and to a successful survey.

The survey: issues and tips

All organisations – and indeed often departments, sections and staff within the organisation – have different histories, structures, objectives, procedures and problems. The records manager will need to be curious, persistent, reassuring, sensitive (to the reasons people might be resistant to the survey) and above all else an excellent communicator to ensure the survey is successful.

Issues

Whatever the nature of the institution, the most common problem faced by the record surveyor is difficulty identifying record series. Institutions and departments frequently organise their records into large groups arranged by subject or correspondent, but not according to easily identifiable series. Where this is the case, it may be necessary to spend additional time reviewing the records. There may be several series buried in one arrangement, or it may be that one series runs across various groups of records (e.g. exhibition records in different departments). Identifying the series is important for establishing retention periods and ultimately gaining control over the records.

Tip

Remember, *records series* are groups of records arranged in accordance with a filing system or managed as a unit because they relate to a particular subject, or function, and result from the same activity.

Another issue likely to be encountered is where records are stored in no discernible arrangement, but rather have simply been dumped or discarded in boxes and files or on shelves. In this case it can be very difficult to identify series, or indeed to see any order at all. Do not be put off by the initial sight of the problem. The material may not be as chaotic as it appears. Sometimes records stored in this manner have simply been removed from their original containers or location due to lack of space in another storage environment. Records that have been treated in such a manner are likely to be inactive. It is probable that their current counterparts are better managed elsewhere in the institution. For this reason, chaotic record storage areas are best left until last on the survey agenda. It is easy to become sidetracked by sorting out such material, and time spent identifying record series in this environment might be wasted if similar records are later located elsewhere. When reviewing these areas at the end of the survey, make some rules.

- Allocate how much time can be spent trying to identify record series, and stick to it.

- Pick a selection of files and papers, and try to identify whether the records belong to a series already identified. If they do not, make a note of the creating body, subject matter and date range of the records. It may be possible to associate them with an existing series at a later date.

- Measure the space occupied by the unidentified, unsorted material.

- *Do not* spend time sorting the area as part of the survey.

- *Do* calculate roughly how long it will take to sort the material and present the results as an option or recommendation for future action in the final survey or action report.

Approaching areas of chaotic, unsorted records in this way will help ensure that the survey finishes to deadline. It will also highlight the extent of the problems facing the institution, and begin to suggest that records management is an ongoing requirement. In addition, the process of sorting out a record dumping ground – if managed as a recognised post-survey project – can present a very useful promotion opportunity clearly demonstrating the value of records management to the institution.

Interviews

Whether the direct or the devolved survey methodology is employed, it will be necessary to interview staff. The extent of this activity will vary depending on the aims and scope of the survey and the size of the institution, but it is likely that for many staff the survey interview will represent their first direct encounter with records management, so the records manager must ensure this experience is a positive one. There are no hard-and-fast rules for conducting survey interviews, but the following basic pointers may help.

- Be clear – start by explaining the purpose of the survey and the interview. Ensure all questions are straightforward. Rephrase questions as many times as necessary until they are understood.

- Listen – give the interviewees time to respond to the questions and let them answer in their own words. Do not prompt or suggest answers.

- Verify – where responses are unclear, verify until the meaning is understood.

- Stick to the questionnaire – do not get sidetracked on to other issues or involved in detailed analysis of records or organisational problems.

- Stick to the time allocated – do not let interviews run over the scheduled time available. A maximum length of an hour is recommended. Any longer than this and the interview will become unprofitable and staff will have a hard time clearing space in their diaries. Remember that running over time may be bad publicity for the survey.

- Remain neutral – do not make judgements about records and filing systems. Doing so will alienate staff. Do be sympathetic to the issues they raise.

- Be helpful – the purpose of records management is to improve record systems for everyone. Make sure the interviewee is aware of this. If it is appropriate to do so, offer quick solutions to problems. Do not wait until the survey process is over if simple guidance can be provided immediately.

- Follow up – when notes from the interview have been written up, present a copy to staff. Invite them to identify any errors and make comments; but do not necessarily wait beyond a firm deadline before issuing the final version, as it may take some time for responses to come in.

Tip

In addition to the standard survey questionnaire, it is useful to ask the following open-ended questions of your colleagues.

- What problems do you experience with current record systems?

- What elements of records keeping would you like to change or improve?

Compiling data

The survey process will yield a great deal of information, and it is vital that this is recorded fully and accurately as the survey progresses. Notes from interviews or visits to departments should ideally be written up at the end of the same day, as impressions and nuances quickly fade. Likewise, if interviews proceed quickly, the resulting notes are often scribbled and cursory. These should be written up as soon as possible to avoid ambiguity and misinterpretation at a later date. Similarly, survey forms should be reviewed and the data entered into the survey tool as soon as they are complete. It is easier to follow up any queries that may arise if these are identified immediately.

Tip

It is tempting to bring a laptop to interviews and enter data throughout discussions. However, taking notes (on a questionnaire template) with a pen and clipboard is usually a better approach. The process is less intimidating to staff, and writing notes up after the event allows for full concentration during data collection and time for reflection after the event.

Ideally the survey process should produce:

- a report for each area/section/department summarising the current situation, highlighting any problems and making preliminary recommendations for improved practice
- detailed data (recorded in spreadsheet/database, etc.) identifying record series, format, location, extent, dates, etc.

It may be useful to keep, and regularly review, a daily list of totals. This will help ensure that the data collected remain manageable and understanding of the overall record-keeping situation grows as the survey progresses. The data collection system (database, spreadsheet, etc.) should be able to calculate such totals with ease, but it will need to be programmed accordingly. It may be useful to compile daily tallies for the following:

- volume of active records
- volume of inactive records
- volume in paper format
- volume/amount in electronic format.

Communicate

From start to finish, the process of conducting a record survey is likely to be lengthy. To keep up momentum for records management during this period and ensure that staff remain engaged with the project, it is very important to provide regular feedback and progress reports to relevant stakeholders. Do not labour this process. Only report when there is something worth saying, but do make sure that staff are aware of key developments. At the very least, present each department/section with a summary of the survey findings when work in their area is complete.

Tip

It may be helpful to provide updates during the course of the survey via the following channels:

- all-staff e-mails where appropriate
- articles or snippets in the staff newsletter
- postings on the museum intranet
- agenda items at departmental meetings and heads of department meetings
- staff talks/presentations
- executive reports to senior management.

Above all, try to ensure that every staff interaction during the survey is positive; the aim is to provide help and demonstrate that records management will benefit the museum.

Post-survey: analyse, summarise and report

For the survey to be a success, the data returned must be analysed and evaluated and the findings presented to senior management. Since records management is meant to improve records and information systems for the whole institution, take care not to become sidetracked with detailed data analysis, but rather focus on establishing a global view. A survey that only results in statistical information is not a useful one. The aim when examining the data should be to establish the state of record keeping across the entire institution. The report should identify problems, establish priorities and make recommendations for improved practices in the future.

Data analysis

If data have been collected effectively, it should be easy to compile a comprehensive summary of all the records being created and managed by the institution. This should include, for each record series, details of:

- location
- format
- volume
- usefulness (how long they are active)
- legal requirements

- value (are they required for the archive?)
- status (are they *vital records*?).

This information will form the foundation of the records management programme. Using the information collected, it will be possible to start developing key records management tools, including the retention schedule and file plan (see Chapter 7), as well as supporting best practice across the museum.

If questions have been carefully compiled, it should also be possible to manipulate data in order to extract more complex results that quantify the scale of different problems. For example:

- note number of vital records (Q15) kept in unsecured storage (Q17)
- note volume of records containing personal data (Q12) kept in unsecured storage (Q17).
- what records are of archive value (Q21), and are these kept in prime office/data storage space (Q8)?

This type of analysis is useful because it identifies 'quick-win' projects which can be rolled out immediately following the survey and will clearly demonstrate the value of records management. It is also useful over the longer term when drawing up a more detailed action plan and securing the resources to support it.

This is also why 'Can you find the records and information you need easily; if not, why not?' is one of the most important questions in the survey. Not only does it provide key data about systems (or lack thereof), it also points towards problem areas that are often relatively easy to address, thus illustrating the importance of records management to the museum.

Final report

When a global view of the situation in the institution has been determined and key issues identified, a forward plan of action can be developed. This needs to be communicated to senior management; the best method of doing so is via a formal report. The survey process is likely to take considerable time to complete and involve input from across the institution, so it is important that the report reflects this. The document should summarise the findings of the survey in a clear, concise manner. It should identify existing good practice as well as problems or issues, assess the risks, make recommendations for improved practice and finally present a proposed plan of action setting out how the recommendations will be achieved.

Tip

Suggested section headings for a final survey report are as follows.

- Background (to the survey, why was it implemented).
- Methodology (how were the data collected).
- Summary of record-keeping situation in the institution.
- Specific problems of note and good practices in place.
- Implications of the existing record-keeping situation.
- Recommendations and improvements.
- Plan of action (can be a summary but should indicate timeframes, e.g. one, two, three years, etc.).
- Next steps.

The ultimate aim of the report should be to communicate the existing situation to senior management, giving them enough information to approve the plan of action so that the task of implementing a records management programme can begin. Above all, the report should be factual and helpful rather than critical. It should clearly demonstrate how records management will address the identified issues and how it will benefit the museum.

Tip

The survey process should take no longer than one-quarter of the time allotted to the overall project, records management pilot, business objective period, etc. The remaining time should be spent implementing recommendations.

6

Strategy and action planning

Sarah R. Demb

Abstract: Discusses why and how to develop a records management strategy and an action plan, including linking records management to the wider museum strategy, and how to plan for required staff, equipment, space and supplies resources.

Key words: strategy, action plan, implementation plan, resources.

Introduction

Records management should link to strategic and action planning at a corporate or museum-wide level. This allows for implementing the records management programme according to a structured plan with the cooperation of senior management and colleagues.

Although the focus of this book is records management, this chapter includes some planning for the resources needed to prepare records for the archival end of their life cycle, as some records managers may be charged with this task. However, most of the resource planning focuses on what is needed for active and inactive records.

Why to plan

Museums are busy organisations with many deadline-critical activities such as exhibitions, capital (building) projects and fundraising. Records management must not only be *recognised as an essential function* to save museum resources, but also *built into the way the museum develops its own culture*. To this end, most museums have a 'forward' or strategic plan that follows a set of strategic objectives which allow them to address areas of weakness, build on areas of strength, identify priorities and relevant resources and adapt to changing customer or patron bases. Records management activities should be integrated into this *overall planning process*.

The point of the museum's forward or strategic plan is not just to document its management activities, but also to follow a *consistent process* by which to achieve medium- and long-term goals. Many forward plans follow a three- to five-year cycle and are often updated annually.

Although records management is an ongoing core function of the museum, its initial phases are often conceived of – and funded – as a *project*. Sometimes a project is the precursor to making a business case for ongoing support of a full-fledged records management *programme*. The risk is that museum staff may assume that records management will be completed at the end of the project, when in fact the main goal is to establish it as a core function of the museum. It should be made clear from the beginning that records management is never a 'one-off' activity, and that in order to embed it as a core function it will need ongoing support and ownership.

Tip

It is critical that records management is included in your museum's formal strategy for its planning cycle (usually three to five years).

Detailed action planning allows for determining an overall *strategy* to progress records management as part of the larger corporate strategic planning process. It should balance what the museum wants to achieve with a realistic sense of what is achievable in the available timeframe known from the outset. Explore whether it is best to frame the start-up as a project or an ongoing programme; this will depend on the institutional culture of the museum.

Tip

If there are a large number of tasks to progress and goals to achieve across many museum departments or sections, and no additional staff time to help out, consider running a pilot project with one discrete unit as a starting point to evaluate your methodology. This will ensure that you learn what works and what needs to be adapted to local context early on.

How to plan

The key to making these activities into a coherent programme lies in the information collected through the *records survey or assessment* detailed in Chapter 5. The information acquired about the strengths and weaknesses in records keeping at the museum contains the raw data needed to prioritise the next steps: what issues need to be addressed in order to define goals and achieve them.

List these issues, along with the solutions (next steps) and the people responsible for addressing them in an action plan that details the timeframe within which they need to be addressed. Merely listing the issues like this also helps to refine priorities. (See Chapter 8 for links to a sample action plan and strategy documents.)

The plan should be a working document to help set objectives and prioritise tasks, and will change over time. It is a tool to link records management objectives with organisational priorities and keep the implementation manageable.[1] Once priorities are defined, it is worth taking another look at the scale of the programme. Be realistic. How long will it take to get a records management programme fully up and running?[2]

A plan should link overall programme objectives (which in turn may support the museum's strategic objectives) to goals that are achieved by measurable actions within specific timeframes. The programme objectives may have more than one goal, and those goals may require more than one action or task to achieve the overall objective.

It is helpful for the stated timeframes to relate to the specific actions rather than the objectives, but read as a whole the document will provide a picture of what needs to happen over the medium to long term in order to put good records management into practice in the museum.

Figure 6.1 shows a strategic plan template[3] for a sample objective.

| **Figure 6.1** | Records management programme action plan template |

Objective	Goal/s	Action/s	Timeframe
1. To keep proper records of museum activities	A. Reduce duplication of records on shared drives by agreeing a museum file plan	■ Review shared drive of pilot team ■ Draft file plan and agree ■ Implement file drive clean-up according to plan	[Quarter 1 of financial year] [Quarter 2 of financial year] [Quarter 3 of financial year]

How to make the plan into a strategy

The combination of defining goals to achieve within a reasonable timeframe and agreeing the steps to achieving them comprises the *strategy*. A records management strategy should take into account any concurrent museum-wide or very large initiatives, so as to plan how resources can be deployed effectively and support those initiatives if possible for a 'win-win' situation.

Tip

If a large capital project is about to begin, build records keeping into the project process from the start, thereby lightening a lot of the work from the outset and illustrating the benefits of records management to colleagues.

Keep in mind any other initiatives to ensure that the strategy will complement larger organisation-wide goals. The strategy should also inform the museum's main strategic or forward plan. A mandate for records management should ensure a 'seat at the table'; a means to input to the larger planning process. This in turn should provide some control over the pace of establishing records management within the constraints of the museum's resources and forward plan.

Tip

Putting effort into all this work at the start means that you can be proactive – rather than reactive – to records management issues, and you will have a clear idea of what is feasible when colleagues come to you for advice and assistance.

It is easy to feel overwhelmed by the scale of records management issues when previous record-keeping practices have been *ad hoc*. The planning process should provide practical tools to stave off this situation and help to address the issues in a systematic way.

Planning for required resources

The initial investment the museum makes in records management can be relatively *resource heavy*, although many museums already have what is needed: basic supplies, any non-office records storage space, physical storage equipment (racking), staff (even one person) and funds for all these items. If money is already being spent on records management activities, it is important that a specific budget (or budgets) is identified as such – or that records management becomes a line item in administrative budgets. In Chapter 3 we made clear that set-up costs can be calculated ahead of time as part of the business case, and are often outweighed by savings. Below is an outline of suggested resources needed to begin and maintain a programme so as to help cost and budget them.

Storage space for paper and electronic records

Records storage space is critical to records management. No matter how much backlog is disposed of, staff will still need to refer to active records; some inactive records need to be kept for legal or regulatory reasons; and some records will have archival value and need to be kept permanently. Whether these records are in paper or electronic formats, you will need to address how they are stored. (See also Chapter 7, where criteria for these decisions are scoped in more detail.)

> **Tip**
>
> Is there available space for a records centre (where records can be stored once they are no longer needed in offices, but before they are disposed of) or archive (long-term records storage)? Use the records survey data on the rate at which certain types of records increase annually to calculate and plan for storage space growth rates.

The space resources available to you may determine the type of records management programme you establish, even if this changes over time as more resources become available.

Physical custody of records

As previously mentioned, one of the most useful 'quick wins' of a records management programme is to take physical custody of inactive or 'semi-current' paper records identified in the survey – this means freeing up office space by removing inactive records to a records store (often part of a museum archive store).

Intellectual custody of records

If there is not the space to take custody of paper records, the programme can simply focus on the 'intellectual' side of records management via the development and implemenation of file plans and retention schedules, and provision of advice on best practice (addressed in the next chapter).

Hybrid physical and intellectual custody of records

If there is limited records storage space available, consider offering a *hybrid programme* in which some departments physically manage their own inactive and archival records (often sensible for teams like finance where clear retention periods are mandated by law and where the majority are eventually disposed of), and other departments deposit their inactive and archival records (especially sensible for records that need a review date to look at whether they have long-term or permanent value, such as certain curatorial and exhibition records).

Ensure that any records store space is appropriate. Historically, museums have had a tendency to keep paper records in the basement or the attic, both of which are vulnerable to flooding/leaks, pests and other environmental damage. Active and inactive paper records need to be stored in an area that is at low risk from flood and fire. Servers containing electronic records must be in a climate-controlled environment at a consistent temperature; resources for this may be problematic for smaller museums. Long-term requirements for archival records in electronic formats are addressed in Chapter 7.

Tip

If there is no or limited on-site storage space for the records you need to keep, are there funds for a suitable off-site store, whether owned by the museum or a commercial vendor? Investigate costs and services accordingly. Keep in mind that you will probably have to pay for each retrieval request. How often do you anticipate needing to access materials stored off site? See Chapter 8 for resources for evaluating off-site records storage.

Archive records on paper should be stored in a controlled environment similar to the way objects are stored, according to British Standard 5454 which sets out temperature and humidity ranges for document storage, along with shelving schemes and document container specifications (see Chapter 8 for records storage standards and procedures). Further guidance on the storage of archival records is provided by TNA's Advisory Service.

Ad hoc storage decisions for records often occur when an exhibition space becomes available or a major capital project forces the records manager's hand – it is better to plan ahead even if space is not immediately available.

Remember that on-site space is essential to prepare records for off-site storage, so a long worktable for paper records preparation and a computer workstation are minimum requirements, along with a limited amount of racking for boxes. If the museum uses 'hot-desks', ensure there is access to a worktable and a suitable trolley for transporting boxes of paper records.

Tip

If you cannot immediately afford or do not have access to a space suitable for racking, ensure paper records are stored off the floor in file cabinets or in boxes on pallets to prevent or reduce any damage from soiling, flooding or leaking at the floor level (see Chapter 8 for futher details on environmental control for records storage). Encourage proper care of records in office space by helping staff to gain control of piles of paper and old computer disks.

The increasing cost-effectiveness of computer memory is a double-edged sword of sorts – *do* invest in more memory to speed up systems and ensure that the records needed for the long term are not lost to clear-ups, but be aware that good records management does not adhere to the 'memory is cheap, let's keep everything' ethos. Records identified for disposal or archives in your retention schedule should not be segregated by format. Keep or dispose of records *according to their content*, not their media. Remember that when the FOIA applies to the museum, it covers all formats of records equally, so the museum is obligated to apply its records schedule to electronic records. Unless the schedule specifies that the museum will 'keep everything' then it violates the FOIA by doing so for electronic records. Simply adding more memory to servers is a quick fix, not a quick win, and will merely cause records management problems in the near future.

Planning for staffing needs

All records managers or museum staff who have designated responsibility for records management rely on the assistance of their colleagues. Records management is everyone's responsibility. However, depending on the size and complexity of the museum, and whether records management is the whole or part of one job description, it may be wise to formalise additional staff help.

Sometimes this help is just half an hour to an hour spent talking with each selected colleague during the records survey – this initial investment may help to avoid drains on staff time to help identify records later on.

As agreed in the records management policy discussed in Chapter 4, it is advisable to add records management tasks to performance management reviews of targeted key staff – often department administrators or personal assistants – and at a broad level to senior management job descriptions. Consider establishing records management 'liaison' staff, 'lead users' or a working group/committee made up of appropriate staff, and take this forward under the remit of the action plan.

Refer to the records management policy and work with human resources or personnel officer/s to ensure that the responsibilities it defines are reflected in performance management reviews. This keeps records management at the forefront of staff consciousness across the museum and delegates responsibility in a way that makes records management work for everyone.

Tip

If you can afford an assistant, hire one! However, in budget-scarce times you may need to consider alternatives, such as supervising an intern. Many students on records and archive or museum studies courses must complete practicums or work experience for credits, so you can impart valuable skills that enable them to complete their courses and you to move your records management programme ahead. It is important that interns have discrete, well-defined tasks that can be completed in one term or less.

Contact professional organisations and listservs to identify people or university programmes with an interest in pursuing records management or museum archives as a career (see Chapter 8 for relevant resource links).

Do not underestimate the time it takes to train and supervise interns properly – and to evaluate their work

---

to give feedback in a constructive way. Even if you have to start on your own, it is good to think ahead about what kind of help you might want if you could resource it. Year 2 or 3 of your programme may be the best time for interns to join you.

If your museum has a volunteer pool, consider whether any of your tasks, such as identifying people in photographs or repackaging records, might be done by volunteers, including your 'Friends of the Museum' group. However, do remember that unless yours is an all-volunteer museum, volunteers do not normally carry out work that would require a professional qualification or degree.[4] Additionally, volunteers will require as much, if not more, training and management commitment as your regular staff and interns, so build this into your programme.

Take into account what tasks can be achieved without extra assistance; will you need help just to get started? Determine the extent of staff help available and what can be realistically requested of colleagues. Know if staff help will be paid or unpaid. Map out how much time is needed from colleagues, e.g. flag some time at senior management meetings, or approach colleagues in facilities ahead of time about any anticipated expertise needed from that depatrment in terms of space/storage planning and fitting out.

Planning for supplies and equipment

The supplies and equipment needed will depend on the type of records management programme offered. Basic supplies consist of boxes to pack records in, and pencils to label boxes and folders where necessary. Boxes can be bought from the museum's usual stationer or office supply vendor.

It is important to address whether:

- records storage boxes are of a standard size so they will fit on shelving and be comfortable to lift/move; it is easy to overpack outsized boxes only to find they are too heavy to lift without risk to staff health and safety
- there is adequate racking or pallets for storage of records boxes
- there is a ready supply of basics like pencils and folders
- each department will supply what is required and what will be supplied centrally – how will this impact on budgets?
- there is sufficient server space to deal with certain electronic records (such as high-resolution images) over time.

To address the preservation needs of archival records, make a list of supplies and equipment and find out which vendors provide the specialist materials needed. Confer with the conservation department or colleagues on a conservation listserv to discover any available preferred rates. A *supplies checklist template* with space to fill in costs and add items is given in Appendix 11.

Notes

1. See *www.museuminfo-records.org.uk/toolkits/Records Management.pdf* (accessed: 31 December 2010).
2. It is unlikely that it will take less than three years, although it is possible to achieve many useful 'quick wins' during this time, and museums with a very small staff may find that one year is feasible.

3. A fuller sample action plan is available at *www.museuminfo-records.org.uk/docs/sample_implementation_plan.doc* (accessed: 31 December 2010).
4. See *www.mla.gov.uk/what/programmes/renaissance/regions/london/News_and_Resources/volunteer_training_bank* (accessed: 31 December 2010).

7

Developing a file plan, retention schedule and records management programme

Charlotte Brunskill

Abstract: Explores how to develop and implement a file plan and record retention schedule in both electronic and paper environments. Examines the practical issues involved in using these tools to establish a records management programme.

Key words: file plan, retention schedule, policy, EDRMS, digital environment, electronic records.

Introduction

As established in Chapter 1, *records management is a set of tools that enables museum staff to retrieve the right information in the right format at the right time at the lowest possible cost* (Wythe, 2004: 112). Subsequent chapters have explored the conceptual context and the background information required to help prepare a records management programme. This chapter examines the key tools required to implement that programme: the file plan and records retention schedule. It also examines an important practical issue: how to approach the physical management of records. For the most part, the advice in this chapter is relevant to both paper and electronic records. However, in some instances the different formats have distinct requirements. Where this is the case, format-specific guidance is provided.

In addition, this chapter focuses on delivering electronic records management via a shared drive or network. This is not the only means of securing control over e-records: electronic document and records management systems (EDRMS) provide an alternative. EDRMS are databases designed to support the creation, management and delivery of electronic content, documents and records. However, not only are these systems usually expensive, they are also more suited to large-scale operations in which rigid corporate record-keeping rules can be applied. The working procedures needed to support such systems are generally over-complex for most museums. It is also now widely recognised that the principles and practices which must be developed and implemented to secure management of electronic records via a shared drive are relevant to the introduction of EDRMS. Specifically, any institution wanting to gain control over its electronic records – regardless of the operating environment employed to facilitate this – *must* develop and implement a corporate file plan and best practice guidance for naming records and version control. The advice in this chapter is thus relevant to all electronic environments.

The file plan

The file plan is not a new records management concept. Before the advent of mass computerisation, it was the key tool employed to help organise paper records. Traditionally, the file plan identified the different functional sections of an organisation and, underneath these functions, listed the major types, or series, of records created and held. Essentially, it was intended as a guide for filing. By grouping similar types of information together according to the main business functions and activities of the institution, records were easier to find. The file plan also established records as a corporate resource with all staff (at least in theory) filing and retrieving records from a single shared system. In some institutions, file plans were quite formal, often operating and known as 'registered filing systems'. In others they were less official, with staff adding records to recognised but not rigidly observed structures.

Over the last 20 years, however, as computers became common in the workplace, file plans lost favour and individual record-keeping practices proliferated. It is only relatively recently that their value has been rediscovered. Without a recognised filing structure in place, the organisation of electronic records soon becomes chaotic. In fact, for this reason they are perhaps almost more useful in an electronic environment than they are for managing paper records. A file plan can help deal with the following common electronic record-keeping problems:

- increase of folders on the shared drive
- duplication of information (i.e. the same record held in many different folders)
- chaotic filing structures (in which staff find it difficult to locate information of relevance).

In principle, a file plan for 'born-digital' records should look exactly the same as one for paper records and be employed consistently across both formats. The top level of the structure should reflect the museum's main business functions. The subfolders underneath might include, at different levels, a combination of activities, team functions and record series. The file plan simply agrees these different groupings/folder titles with staff and thereby establishes a corporate structure into which all records can be filed.

In a paper environment, the file plan is primarily an intellectual construct used by the records manager to help establish a corporate view of the many record series created and managed by an institution. It may not necessarily 'exist' in a single identifiable form, but will be represented in the various tools (including retention schedules, best practice documents and so on) employed by the records manager. Although it might be desirable for individual staff to understand the entire filing structure of their institution, this is not always necessary in practice. In larger institutions, which encompass many functions and produce hundreds of record series, staff ultimately need only an awareness of how to manage the records for which they are responsible.

However, in an electronic environment the situation is different. Many institutions now manage records via a 'shared drive'; where this is the case, staff are normally presented with a view of the entire network structure (represented by folders and subfolders) of the organisation and required to determine where to file their records within it. Although it is possible to block folders from view or provide staff with shortcuts to relevant areas, this becomes time-consuming and problematic as settings continually need to be updated when staff leave or take on new tasks. In an electronic environment, it is therefore vital that staff have an understanding of the corporate structure: how the records they create fit into the whole. This will enable them not only to file electronic records appropriately, but also to navigate the shared drive to locate and retrieve records of relevance. This is most important if the communal working facilities of the shared drive – specifically, the ability to share records readily (a facility not available in the same way in a paper environment) – are to be maximised. Unlike the paper environment, when creating an electronic document staff need to consider 'How does this record fit into the whole?' This represents an enormous culture change: in an electronic environment, all record creators must also become to some extent record keepers.

For this reason, a recognised file plan is the key to successful management of electronic records. Constructing and implementing a file plan suitable for twenty-first-century business practices incorporating both paper and electronic records can be a complex exercise, not least because it requires the involvement of staff across the entire organisation. The following steps are recommended.

Step 1: Background research

The first step is to review how paper records have historically been managed in the institution. Although it might appear that there is no formal structure in place, closer inspection could reveal that records have been organised according to particular types. If a record survey has been conducted, review the data collected – are there any patterns or groupings that emerge? If the museum employs an archivist, speak to them about how historic records have been arranged. Examine the archive catalogue, if there is one, to determine universal language and themes that might be applicable across current business. Above all, try and take the widest view. This will help determine the functions that the institution has consistently undertaken. It is important that the system developed is both future-proof and transparent.

Having examined the historic arrangement of the institution's records, look at how they are currently organised. How does the museum manage its 'born-digital' records? Relevant information might have been identified during the record survey process if this encompassed shared-drive spaces. It will be useful to review this during the process of file plan development. The following questions should be considered.

- What does the top level of the shared drive say about the work the museum carries out; what common themes or groupings can be identified?

- What information is filed on the shared drive? How has this been arranged?

Having established both how the institution managed its records historically and how it manages them currently, the two systems should be compared. Is it possible to determine any series groupings or patterns that are consistent across both? Even if on the surface it appears that records are unmanaged, on closer inspection it is likely that some type of order exists. Most record creators arrange their records according to their own kind of logic. It may be that only the very loosest of structures can be identified, but this is still relevant. It is important to avoid reinventing the wheel. Not only will this save a lot of work, but by basing the file plan on patterns that already exist across historic and current record arrangements, the structure developed will be both understood and used by staff. It is also more likely to be future-proof.

It is a good idea to look at file plans in other similar organisations.[1] Although there will always be differences, the core business of most museums and galleries is remarkably similar. Figure 7.1 suggests seven 'top-level' functions – or record groups – that are common in the sector.

Depending on the size of the institution, it may not be necessary to include all the top-level functions listed in Figure 7.1. Similarly, some functions will have more subsets of activities (and result in more records series) than others.

Figure 7.1 Top-level museum/gallery functions

Records group (top-level museum functions)	Relevant activities that create records series
Governing the museum/governance (decision-making bodies)	Boards and board committees, directorate and staff committees, policy development, business planning and strategy, audit and risk management
Managing resources/operations	Personnel, facilities, buildings and grounds, security, finance and procurement, information technology, information governance, including records management and institutional archives
Managing collections	Acquiring, appraising, registering, documenting, cataloguing, conserving, loans out and caring for objects of all types, including controlled environments for storage; interpreting objects and collections
Managing commercial activities	Venue hire, catering, publishing, retail operations, picture library (intellectual property)
Organising exhibitions	Interpreting objects, managing exhibition spaces and cases, loans in, and installing objects
Facilitating learning and access	Delivering education and learning programmes relating to exhibitions, collections and wider themes, special events, online collections access (which may cross with managing collections and managing resources)
Developing external relations	Media relations, corporate and individual membership, community relations and other fundraising

The activities or key records series listed reflect the work carried out by museum staff. While some activities concern a single functional area (e.g. *Loans in* records can only be found under the *Organising exhibitions* function), others relate to several records groups (e.g. most functions include policy creation). The question to answer from a records management point of view is whether it is appropriate for the shared drive to include a number of different policy folders, or whether the museum would benefit from a single 'master file' in which all these policies reside. If the latter is preferable, where should that master file live? The answer will probably be determined by which job role has ultimate responsibility for those policies – and if more than one role has responsibility, then those files might live outside the relevant team directories or folders. Other similar problem areas are likely to include finance records and best practice or procedural documents.

Chapter 8 contains further information on sample file plans.

Step 2: Consultation with colleagues

Once the record-keeping patterns and structures that already exist in the institution and the sector are determined, the task of developing the file plan can begin in earnest. There are two ways to approach this.

- Draft the new proposed structure independently (based on the review work carried out) and then consult with selected colleagues to agree the final plan.

- Conduct interactive workshop sessions in which the existing structure is reviewed and a file structure is drafted with selected museum staff or teams.

The chosen approach will probably depend on the size of the organisation, the timeframe available and the number of staff on hand to assist with the work. If the workshop method is preferable, the following steps are recommended.

- Hold a preliminary session to ensure staff understand exactly what a file plan is and the benefits it can bring the institution.

- Organise a workshop session in which staff address the question 'What does our institution do?' All answers, from the grand (e.g. builds an understanding of national identity through portraits) to the small scale (e.g. serves tea in the café), are acceptable. Encourage staff to be open. Write the responses on 'sticky notes'; when no further ideas are forthcoming, arrange the sticky notes into like groups. Ensure each group has a heading. While it is important the records manager or person facilitating the session is informed about sector-relevant file plans, do not circulate or discuss examples with colleagues beforehand.

- Write up the sticky notes into a draft file plan and circulate to staff.

Whether the file plan has been drafted independently or constructed with staff, allow plenty of time for feedback.

Tip

Never impose a file structure on colleagues – if they have not been involved in its development, it is likely to appear alien and they will avoid using it.

Step 3: Implementing the file plan

As discussed earlier, the file plan should remain consistent across all record formats. Although it may not 'exist' in a single identifiable form in a paper environment, in an electronic environment it is likely to be visible to all staff, as represented by the folders and subfolders of the shared drive. Consequently, while the 'top levels' of a paper file plan are largely intellectual constructs employed by the records manager, and therefore can be renamed or redesigned with little impact on staff, in an electronic environment quite the opposite is true. Staff across the institution will use the high levels of the file plan on a daily basis, and in order to ensure they can easily do so, various best practices have emerged.[2] In an electronic environment the following are recommended.

- There should be a maximum of seven to ten folders at each level.

- There should be a maximum depth of four to five subfolders ('clicks') before the records themselves are reached.

- All records should reside at the same 'level' (number of clicks down).

- Permissions should be 'locked down' for at least the first two levels (so that only agreed 'super-users' are able to add new folders). This is so that at these top levels the folder structure remains constant, enabling staff to become familiar with the route or file path they need to take to get to the records.

The principles detailed above represent current best advice in the field of electronic records management. However, they are not absolute rules and some may be difficult to implement and sustain in a working environment. All file plans should be constructed in a manner that is sympathetic to the institution. For example, if the museum is small, it may not be necessary to introduce four or five folder levels. It is important to liaise closely with the IT department throughout the entire process. In particular, setting folder permissions is often guided by the specific network and systems parameters in an institution.

Before implementing the new structure it is important to determine whether it is appropriate to 'close' the existing structure and start again entirely from scratch, or to review the contents of the existing structure and attempt to rationalise and refile records retrospectively according to the best practice introduced.

The route taken will depend on the situation in the institution. If the shared drive is extensive and chaotic, it may be sensible to begin again. Working with the IT department, establish a 'D-Day' date from which point staff will no longer be able to add records to the old shared drive and all new business must be conducted in the new network space according to new best practice. In this instance *active records* – those required for everyday business – should be transferred over to the new structure. 'Read-only' access to the expired network space should remain (ensuring that staff can see the contents of the old shared drive, but not add to it).

If the museum is small, and the contents and order of the shared drive are relatively manageable, it may be preferable to rationalise and refile the contents. Reordering a shared-drive space might also tie in with the recommendations made in the initial record survey report. If this route is chosen, the following must be addressed.

- Duplicate records – does the network contain many copies of the same records? Does it contain folders with the same title? These records must be rationalised wherever possible.

- Draft records – does the network contain drafts, notes or early versions of material later finalised? These are records that can usually be deleted.

- Expired records – does the network contain records which are no longer active (such as old minutes or reports). These records might be moved to cheaper near-line or offline storage (where they are not immediately visible to staff, but can be called back if necessary.) See below for a more detailed explanation.

- Completed records – does the network contain records that can be 'closed' (folders for completed projects or other functions/activities) and made read-only for archive purposes?

- Reference records – if the institution has an intranet, it is useful to identify the records (usually policies and procedures) that staff need to refer to on a regular basis so that they can be made available on the intranet.

If rationalising an existing shared drive, records need to be moved and deleted as appropriate.

Step 4: Support through best practice and training

When the file structure has been finalised, it must be supported by guidance and training for staff. In a paper environment, this is relatively simple: staff need to know how to title and organise files pertinent to their area of work. Training can remain local and specific. In an electronic environment, it is of paramount importance that all staff adhere to the same practices. As such the following are essential.

- Naming conventions – what is the preferred method for titling folders and records?

- Version control – what is the preferred method for managing drafts and different versions of documents?

- E-mail management – how will e-mail be managed? Should e-mails of significance be saved to the shared drive alongside other documents? If so, what format is most appropriate? Or are they best managed over the long term within the e-mail client server?

Without institution-wide agreed practice on the above, shared-drive spaces quickly become chaotic and opaque. An extensive literature in its own right has been written on this subject; since guidance is readily available, the issues are not discussed in detail here (although relevant resources can be found in Chapter 8).

When best practice documents have been developed, it is important to ensure they are understood by staff. Compulsory training sessions, organised with input from IT and personnel staff, present the best means of achieving this. A shared-drive file plan is only successful if all computer users understand how and where to create and save records.

Step 5: Consolidate and review

In a paper environment, the implementation of a file plan can usually be accomplished without much ado. Since staff ultimately need only an awareness of record series titles, and not the overall corporate scheme, the file plan can be introduced gradually, section by section, at a pace suitable to the institution. In the electronic environment, the implementation of a file plan represents a significant culture change. Regardless of whether the revised structure addresses only a small section of museum business or encompasses the entire shared drive, the likelihood is that the change from the old system to the new one will be managed as a 'big bang' event rather than a gradual shift in practices (bearing in mind IT protocols, permissions, network access, etc.). For this reason it is important to ensure that relevant staff (usually the records manager and IT personnel) are on hand and have time to answer any queries that arise, and that staff are aware that the structure is a 'pilot' and they should feed back any queries or problems so that changes can be made where relevant.

It may also be helpful to draw up simple procedures setting out:

- who has overall responsibility for the file plan
- who has permission to add folders at specified levels
- who is responsible for answering staff queries and making changes to the file plan in the longer term.

Bear in mind that developing a file plan is not a one-off activity. It represents the business and functions of the institution, so when these change the file plan must change too. This supports a principle repeatedly stressed throughout this text: introducing records management is not a project with a beginning and end. It is an ongoing requirement.

Tip

The file plan is not set in stone. It should be monitored and adapted to take into account any changes in the business and working practices of the museum.

Finally, the *records management policy* should be amended so that it refers directly to the file plan and other best practice documents, and explicitly states that this is the museum's preferred way of managing its records.

Developing and implementing a file plan is invariably a complex piece of work, especially because it requires a global view of the institution's business and in an e-environment involves at some level all computer users. The process should not be rushed. There are no 'correct' answers and there will always be records that do not fit obviously into the categories that have been determined. In the context of a file plan, the 'square peg in a round hole' scenario is unavoidable. It is important to spend time developing the most user-friendly, transparent structure possible, but bear in mind that – at some point – staff will simply have to learn how to use it, just as they would any software employed by the institution.

Provided the file plan has been thoroughly planned, the benefits will be obvious. In a paper environment these will be realised primarily by the records manager: securing intellectual control over and a corporate view of the records of an institution is essential to the development of a successful records management programme. In an electronic environment, staff are the biggest beneficiaries and will quickly see the virtue of the changes. Agreeing a consistent structure and naming conventions represents good records management, because it allows everyone to access information they need quickly and easily. This will have immediate benefits for existing staff and should also secure a seamless transition and continuity for future post holders. Records created by predecessors will be readily available.

Remember, the foundation of the file plan already exists – it just needs to be moulded into a more consistent and workable structure.

The records retention schedule

Now that the file plan has been developed, work can begin on one of the most important records management tools: the *records retention schedule*. Indeed, all the procedures outlined up to this point lead to the preparation of this document. The records retention schedule is the blueprint by which an institution manages its records. It identifies every record series created by the institution and sets out:

- how long these records should be managed throughout the phases (active and inactive) of their life cycle
- what happens to records at the end of this process (review, destroy or transfer to the archive)
- where they should be stored throughout this process (in offices, records store, servers, archive)
- who has responsibility for records
- on what authority the retention decisions are made.

The process for developing the retention schedule can be accomplished as follows.

Step 1: Establish the structure

As mentioned earlier, the file plan should inform the retention schedule. Specifically, most schedules are organised or have the same layout as their related file plans. In particular, high-level functions or records series should be consistent across both documents. However, it is important to bear in mind that the record series listed in the schedule may not be exactly the same as the record groups in the file plan. The schedule may need to be more granular, because the length of time records are kept is influenced not only by business requirements but also by legislation and regulations, which can be very specific according to record type (for instance, within one series type, legislation may set out different retention periods for subsets of records). Figure 7.2 is an example of how an extract from a retention schedule might be organised.

In this example (with the possible exception of *Registration*), the record groups cut across departments or team functions. Organising the retention schedule according to the high-level functions identified in the file plan, rather than by department, establishes the document as a corporate resource which can be referred to by all colleagues. It also renders the retention schedule future-proof: restructuring and departmental name changes will not necessitate updates.

Figure 7.2   Sample retention schedule (extract)

Record type	Keep in office	Action	Authority
1. Governance – trustees meeting minutes	5 years	Transfer to archives after 5 years	Companies Acts 1985 and 1989
2. Health and safety – accident forms/ reports	Current year + 6 years	Destroy	Health and Safety Act 1974
3. Communications – enquiries from the public; Data Protection Act subject access requests	Current year + 2 years	Destroy	Data Protection Act 1998
4. Registration – loan out files	Permanent	Transfer to archives on return of loan (or keep in registrar's office as appropriate to the museum)	Limitation Act 1980; business requirement

> **Tip**
>
> Some schedules also list what the *office of record* is (i.e. where the authoritative original record should be kept), along with different retention periods for any copies held elsewhere. For example, the originals of invoices are usually kept by the finance team for longer than copies made and retained by staff in offices.

Depending on the nature and size of the museum, the retention schedule may be much more detailed than the file plan.

> **Tip**
>
> It is perfectly acceptable to list record series belonging to the same function together if they have the same retention period (as demonstrated by *Communications* in the schedule in Figure 7.2).

Step 2: Establish retention periods

The retention schedule addresses one of the most significant record-keeping problems faced by institutions: which records should be destroyed and when, and which records should be retained permanently. The retention periods set out in the schedule should be established in accordance with relevant legislation. Where legislation is not applicable, retention periods should be determined by weighing up the cost of retaining the records (i.e. physical storage space and back-up) against the cost of destroying them (i.e. the potential cost of a claim). The key Acts affecting record keeping are discussed in Chapter 4. These provide the foundation for retention decisions.

Developing a records retention schedule covering all the records created by an organisation may seem like a daunting task, but many of the functions carried out by the museum, such as activities related to finance, personnel, IT or health and safety, are generic to all businesses. Best practice schedules for relevant records are already available from a number of sources (see Chapter 8). This standard guidance will need to be adjusted to fit the idiosyncrasies and precise operating environment of the museum, but in general these parts of the schedule need not be compiled from scratch.

It is important to consult with colleagues throughout the process of developing a schedule. Even if legislation establishes that records do not need to be retained beyond a specified number of years, staff in the institution may have good reason for holding on to them beyond this point. Indeed, museums often retain records permanently that in another institution might be subject to scheduled destruction. This is largely because of their continuing value to the museum itself. As discussed in Chapter 3, although it is impossible to give precise figures, of all records created, museums tend to retain approximately 15 per cent permanently. The retention periods established should take into account both legal requirements and the particular business needs of the institution.

Step 3: Secure authority

When the schedule has been compiled and agreed with staff, the final and perhaps most important task is to ensure it has been 'signed off' by a senior member(s) of staff. The purpose of the schedule is to mitigate against risk (so that management of records is informed and appropriate). It also provides the records manager with the authority necessary to carry out the requirements of the role: to manage the records of the museum without constantly having refer back to the record creators. For this to be the case, the schedule must be approved by an appropriately senior staff member.

Neither the file plan nor the retention schedule is an inventory. A records inventory or file list is often useful for recording information about records that are inactive or archival (once they are not being amended or otherwise referred to on a regular basis). To summarise: the *file plan* is a document that sets out a framework for organising, or filing, the institution's records. Staff should refer to it when adding folders or adding documents to folders, on the shared drive or in a paper environment. The *retention schedule* is a document that sets out how long categories of records (rather than individual documents, although there are some exceptions) should be kept, and what should happen to them when they are no longer active.

Implementing a records management programme

The file plan and retention schedule are the tools that sit at the heart of the records management programme. Now that these have been developed, consideration must be given to how the programme will be delivered in practice.

Establishing a records store

One option suitable for *paper records* is for the records manager or designated staff person to take physical custody of the records. What this means in practice is that records are physically transferred to a designated records store when they are no longer actively in use in offices by their creators or collectors. Records review and disposal are managed by the records manager, and until disposal records can be recalled by staff at any time (although once records are designated as having *archival value*, it is best practice for them not to circulate outside a reading room). Depending on the resources available, this practice can be implemented for all of the institution's records or only selected records series. Which series are transferred may depend on a number of factors.

- Available storage space – offices that have very little space may have no choice but to transfer records when they are no longer active (not required for everyday business).

- Value of records – a common practice is to ensure that only those records identified, or likely to be considered, for permanent preservation are transferred out of offices. This ensures that the records with the highest value are stored securely, and when the review period detailed in the retention schedule is reached, this process can be easily undertaken by records management staff.

- Retention period – a common practice is to leave record series that have been assigned a disposal date (those that are definitely not required for permanent preservation) in offices. Since they simply need to be destroyed at an identified date, this process is easily managed by office staff acting in accordance with the retention schedule and/or in consultation with the records manager.

- Records format – as already discussed, records exist in a wide variety of formats, but not all are suitable for physical transfer to a records management store. Electronic records are best managed within the working environment in which they were created. Unless the institution has considered and made provision for the medium- to long-term sustainability of electronic records, there is little point in accepting records saved to disk, USB sticks or other 'fugitive' storage devices. Likewise, records stored on digital media – CDs and DVDs – may be problematic if the institution has not planned how these records will be accessed over time. A common practice in many museums yet to develop comprehensive digital sustainability programmes is to operate a 'hard copy only' policy with regard to which records may be transferred to the records store. However, since the point beyond which it may not be practical to print out even selected hard copies is fast approaching, it is worth considering a digital sustainability plan when taking into account how to store records permanently.[3]

Tip

It is a good idea to establish a policy regarding which record series within the institution will be accepted for transfer to the records store. This will make it easier to decline unsuitable material (and to agree what is unsuitable) and ensure the timely transfer of the records required for the archive.

Most institutions operate a hybrid system that takes into account all of the above, but is also pragmatic. There will always be exceptions to the policy. In some cases, particularly if there is initial resistance to records management, it may be politic to take physical custody of records not normally destined for the records store in order to win goodwill and promote the records management programme. Likewise, if staff are particularly territorial, it may be pragmatic to leave records in their offices.

If there is uncertainty about whether it would be appropriate to establish a designated records store, the following factors should be considered.

- Space – is there enough available to establish a fully functional store? Remember that the store will need to accommodate not only those records already created and currently stored in offices, but those that will be created in the future. The volume of records transferred will increase exponentially usually for at least the first six years, when the first group of records reaches its review period,[4] and often beyond this, as the records management programme develops. Before establishing a store it is a good idea to calculate the estimated annual record growth. This should be relatively straightforward if the records survey has been conducted effectively: identify the record series that will be transferred and determine the volume of records created each year. Remember to take into account that future records may be kept solely in electronic format.

- Staff – are there enough staff available to operate a records management store effectively and efficiently? Remember, the transfer of records is time-consuming: at the very least each box of material will need to be logged. Depending on the exact nature of the system implemented, it may be necessary to carry out some weeding and repackaging (more information on the practicalities of transferring material is given below).

- Service level – establishing a records management store means establishing a retrieval service. If the records manager/management team takes custody of inactive records, these records still 'belong' to record creators until they reach their disposal review date. They will need to be retrieved on request. Are there enough staff available to operate this service? A pilot may establish how often retrieval requests tend to occur.

Tip

It is quite acceptable to ask staff to list and ensure that records are appropriately packaged before transfer. Staff are usually happy to do this for records they have created so long as clear instructions, regarding, for example, the level of detail required for box lists, are communicated.

Pre-transfer

If establishing a records management store is desirable, clear procedures must be established to facilitate the transfer process. It is crucial that record creators take an active role in this process, as described above.

Tip

At the very least, the transfer procedure should include the following rules:

- staff must only transfer record series detailed in the policy document or retention schedule
- only record series with an agreed (i.e. signed off) retention period will be accepted for transfer
- all records must be clearly labelled.

If these three criteria are not met, it will be very time-consuming to manage the records and difficult for staff to retrieve them at a later date.

Establishing procedures that require those staff transferring the records to assist with the process also helps emphasise that the records store is not a quick and easy dumping ground for any old material. Other factors to consider are listed below.

- Will material be weeded for duplicates and ephemera before transfer? If so, who will undertake this work – the records manager or the transferring office?

- Will the material be repackaged (boxed) before transfer? To maximise space on shelves, most records stores house the material in uniform boxes of a consistent size. Who will be responsible for the required repackaging – the records manager or the transferring office? Who will provide these boxes?

- Will the transferring office complete a 'transfer sheet' documenting the contents of the boxes? Or are well-labelled files adequate for the purposes of logging the material (see below for further details)?

- Will the transferring office label the outside of the boxes or will this be undertaken by the records manager post-transfer?

It is a good idea to compile a 'best practice' or 'how to' document summarising the preferred transfer procedure. This is time well spent, since it will enable the records manager to deflect unsuitable transfer requests easily. Sample transfer guidance and forms are available in Appendix 12.

Post-transfer

Once the records have been transferred into the custody of the records store, they still need to be managed. To do this effectively, they should be logged; key data about the material should be recorded. This is most effective when done electronically. Elaborate systems are not necessary: Excel-type spreadsheets or standard databases like Access are both quite adequate. If the institution has a well-established archive, it may already have purchased records management software that can be utilised. The most common archive cataloguing system in the UK, Axiell CALM, has a package (CALM Records) specifically designed for managing the physical transfer of inactive records. However, this kind of application is aimed at large institutions managing a significant volume of records, and may not necessarily be suitable for smaller institutions. Whatever system is selected, the key elements of information that must be recorded are as follows.

- Accession date – recording when the records were transferred. This is usually in the format YYYY/running number for a group of records.

- Unique box number – to facilitate retrieval (usually a running number).

- Record series name – this should correspond to the retention schedule and file plan.

- Box contents – what information is held in the box? If the entire contents concern the same subject, a box title alone might be sufficient (e.g. 'Shop receipts 2010/11'). In most instances, however, it will be necessary to list folder titles. Record the correct level of detail needed to facilitate easy retrieval at a later date.

- Date of records – record the date span of the records in the box. This is normally in the format YYYY–YYYY.

- Transfer body – what office transferred the records?

- Retention period – this should correspond to the retention schedule. For example, +6 years (current year plus six years).

- Action at the end of the retention period – review, destroy or transfer to archive.

- Date of action – when will the records be reviewed, destroyed or transferred to the archive? In some applications, this date will be automatically generated by the system. In others, it may need to be calculated manually.

- Action complete date – date when the action was carried out. Even if a record has been destroyed, it is useful to maintain a record of this. This type of data should never be deleted from the system.

To ensure that adequate transfer information is being recorded, it is a good idea to consider how it may need to be manipulated at a later date. Alongside basic searches identifying material for retrieval, the following requests are likely to be useful.

- Which material is time-expired (has reached its review or destruction date)?

- Which records have been deleted?

- Which departments are transferring the largest volume of material?

- What volume of records was transferred in any one year, and is it increasing or decreasing?

Managing records without a designated store

If it is not feasible to establish a designated records store, it will be necessary to determine which staff will be responsible for managing each record series throughout the 'life-cycle' stages. Who will carry out the actions detailed in the retention schedule? Will destruction and review of records be carried out by the records manager, or by other staff? Whatever is determined, the answer should be clearly communicated to the relevant offices and staff, and detailed in the retention schedule.

Tip

If destruction or review of records will be carried out by non-records-management staff, the records manager will still need to ensure that the action points detailed in the retention schedule are being met. A good way of doing this is to establish 1 January (or another date appropriate to the institution) as the standard action date for each record series and then send out reminders to relevant staff or departments at this time, with follow-up reminders coming a month or so later.

Complex systems are not required to manage the intellectual custody of records. Creating the file plan and retention schedule as basic Word documents is perfectly adequate if this is the only tool to hand. This will not enable the more sophisticated level of control that can be achieved by database systems, but it does secure a basic searchable record of what types of records the institution is creating, where these are being maintained and so on.

Management of electronic records

The processes discussed above concern the physical management of paper records. Electronic records, which exist in a virtual environment, have very different requirements. They should be organised according to the structure established in the file plan, but how best to ensure that they are deleted, reviewed or transferred to the archive in accordance with the provisions of the schedule? There are no absolute answers to these questions, as management of e-records is an evolving discipline and the precise operating environment of the particular institution needs to be taken into account when determining appropriate procedures. The subject is complex and an extensive literature in its own right exists. For this reason, what follows is a very general summary of the key issues.

Deletion and review of e-records

If e-records have been organised effectively according to a well-considered file plan (into defined record series, grouped by year or by subject), it should be relatively easy to manage the deletion of those records identified for disposal at a set point. EDRMS can be configured to manage the process automatically. In a shared-drive environment, the task must be assigned to a role or roles. Depending on the size of the institution, this may be sensibly undertaken by the records manager where the institution is small, or liaison staff in each functional area in larger organisations where the management of processes can be hugely time-consuming for one individual.

Where deletion of e-records is a devolved responsibility, it is expedient to amend job descriptions accordingly. This will help emphasise the fact that management of e-records is a corporate responsibility, and that the process has time implications. Even in cases where deletion is managed by liaison staff, the records manager will still need to play a supervisory role, monitoring the network to check that the work is being carried out in a timely and appropriate fashion. In all cases, IT personnel should be involved: the deletion of e-records may not as straightforward as simply clicking the delete button.

Where the action assigned to a record series is 'review', the process should always be undertaken by records management staff, since they have the expertise to determine whether records are required for permanent preservation. This is true regardless of working environment or format (EDRMS, shared drive or paper). Again, if records have been organised effectively, the procedure should be relatively simple.

In both situations, thought will need to be given to whether it is appropriate to store records on the network throughout the semi-active period of the life cycle. Network storage is used for everyday business – it allows frequent, very rapid access to data. However, it is also expensive. Depending on the particular situation of the institution it may not be feasible to store all data online until it is deleted or transferred to an archive.

Instead, IT personnel often advocate moving data to offline or near-line storage. Offline storage involves transferring data to tape or offline disk where it can be retrieved if and when necessary. Near-line storage is an automated system whereby data can be stored on cartridges that can be retrieved from their physical location and loaded remotely by machine. This places data temporarily back online. The disadvantage of offline storage is that storing and retrieving data in this way can be inconvenient and increases the risk of data corruption or loss. Near-line storage is a quicker and more convenient solution (data can be retrieved in just a few seconds), but it is more expensive and may not be feasible in smaller institutions. It should be borne in mind, however, that in both scenarios the removal of data from online storage areas will result in an improved speed of performance for networked data.

Working with IT personnel and taking into account all of the above, the records manager will need to determine whether it is appropriate to retain all data on the network during their active and semi-active periods; or to retain active data on the network but transfer all, or selected, record series to near-line or offline storage when they reach the semi-active stage of the life cycle.

The situation is analogous to a paper environment in which records are stored in prime office space while in everyday use, but may be moved to cheaper off-site storage during the semi-active period of the life cycle. Whatever practices are determined, it is important to record details in the retention schedule.

Tip

It is important to remember that when records are scheduled for deletion, this includes copies on back-up tapes or servers. Legislation like the FOIA dictates that records are managed consistently; there are no exceptions.

Transfer to the archive

Alongside 'destroy' and 'review', the retention schedule includes a third option: transfer to archive. It is important to examine what this entails in the context of electronic records management. Paper records are vulnerable to physical compromise, but if stored appropriately can last for hundreds of years with limited intervention and still remain accessible. The situation in an electronic environment is very different. The preservation of electronic records creates issues from the outset. Problems of technological obsolescence, media fragility and authenticity, if not taken into account at the time of creation, will quickly render the record inaccessible. Securing the permanent preservation of records in this context is complex: it represents perhaps the most challenging issue ever to face the archive profession. An in-depth examination of the subject is not within the intended scope of this book. However, it is worth bearing in mind the following important facts.

- Be aware that the term 'archiving' when used in an IT environment has a completely different meaning to the term as understood by the archive profession. (Briefly, in IT terms 'archiving' simply refers to the offline storage of information – normally for back-up purposes. It is not concerned with securing the comprehensive preservation and accessibility of information over the long term.)

- Migration (transferring records from one generation of computer software to the next), replication (refreshing digital records by copying them on to new media) and emulation (developing archive emulators of software which allow the contents of e-records to be viewed in their original format) are all options for securing digital sustainability, but they require a great deal of consideration and detailed planning – from the point of record creation – to execute successfully.

- Some institutions still operate a 'print-to-paper policy' for archival records. However, advances in technology – the proliferation of e-mail, for instance – means this is fast becoming unrealistic, if not undesirable. In addition, some dynamic records (e.g. databases or CAD systems) cannot be adequately replicated in a paper environment. For these reasons, it is important to begin addressing the situation. This does not need to be on a grand scale: the first stage may simply involve raising awareness.

- The issues surrounding digital sustainability are unavoidable. As the amount of data increases, more and more core business is undertaken in an e-environment; as institutions embrace new technologies, the problem will only be compounded. There are relatively simple ways of reducing future problems; for example, ensuring the institution employs the minimum number of file formats necessary to support business and restricts data creation in non-recognised formats.

The issues are undoubtedly complex, and while answers are unlikely to be readily forthcoming, the problems must not be ignored. For museums, which are often under-resourced and do not have the funds or staff required to develop comprehensive solutions, a sensible approach might involve developing a digital sustainability strategy/programme. This can include an investigation of the issues within the particular operating environment, identification of high-risk areas/records and establishment of possible steps forward. The process of compiling this document will raise awareness, promote understanding and help to ensure a consistent approach across all areas of business.

This chapter has explored how to develop the two essential tools that sit at the heart of records management: the file plan and records retention schedule. It has also examined how a programme might be realised in both paper and electronic environments. It is important to bear in mind, however, that records management is an organic discipline that should be continuously monitored and reviewed. Tools, policies and best practice procedures that have been put in place may need to be altered to reflect any changes in business practice. For records management to reap the rewards outlined – supporting business, managing risk, saving money and resources – it must always remain sensitive to the business needs of the museum.

A final word

The essential steps needed to establish a museum records management programme are as follows.

- *Make a business case and obtain mandate.*
- *Develop policies and procedures* (define responsibilities; integrate into larger context and initiatives via strategic planning; draft framework documents).
- *Obtain the necessary resources* (space, funds and staff).
- *Communicate the programme* (using a variety of forums and 'quick wins').
- *Order supplies and equipment.*
- *Agree workflows with staff.*
- *Implement policies, procedures and practical solutions.*

Some of this is an iterative process. For instance, if the resources to carry out a records survey are available early on, it can help to make the business case and give you a chance to do some 'quick wins' as soon as the records management issues are identified. The steps do not have to occur in the above order, but they must all be implemented at some point. Purchasing some supplies so as to carry out 'quick wins' may come first. Some policies and procedures will necessarily be drafted later on. Like records management itself, it is easier to carry out any initiative in a systematic way. We hope the steps outlined in this book provide a useful route map.

Notes

1. A generic file plan, based on an unpublished prototype for national museums, has been developed for non-nationals and can be found at *www.museuminfo-records.org.uk/toolkits/ RecordsManagement.pdf* (accessed: 31 December 2010).
2. See *www.nationalarchives.gov.uk/documents/managing-electronic-records-without-an-erms-publication-edition.pdf* (accessed: 31 December 2010).
3. The National Archives has produced useful guidance about this subject; see *www.nationalarchives.gov.uk/information-management/guidance/e.htm* (accessed: 31 December 2010).
4. As discussed in Chapter 4, six years is a common retention period assigned to many records series due to UK regulatory requirements.

Resources

Sarah R. Demb

UK legislation and regulations

Data Protection Act 1998
www.legislation.gov.uk/ukpga/1998/29/contents

www.ico.gov.uk/Home/for_organisations/data_protection.aspx

Environmental Information Regulations 2004
*www.defra.gov.uk/corporate/policy/opengov/eir/pdf/
publicity/leaflet-publicauthorities.pdf*

*www.ico.gov.uk/for_organisations/environmental_information
.aspx*

Freedom of Information Act 2000
www.legislation.gov.uk/ukpga/2000/36/contents

*www.ico.gov.uk/for_organisations/freedom_of_information
.aspx*

Local Government Classification Retention Scheme database
of relevant legislation which sets out records retention periods
www.irms.org.uk/lgcrs

Lord Chancellor's Code of Practice on the Management of Records under section 46 of the Freedom of Information Act 2000 (2002)
www.nationalarchives.gov.uk/policy/foi/

Museums and Galleries Act 1992
www.statutelaw.gov.uk/content.aspx?activeTextDocId=2155852

Public Records Act 1958
www.legislation.gov.uk/ukpga/Eliz2/6-7/51

Public Records Act 1967
www.legislation.gov.uk/ukpga/1967/44

Spoliation and repatriation

Spoliation
www.culturalpropertyadvice.gov/spoliation_reports

Repatriation – British Museum
www.britishmuseum.org/the_museum/news_and_press_releases/ statements/human_remains/repatriation_to_tasmania.aspx

Repatriation – Brighton Museum and Art Gallery
www.brighton-hove-rpml.org.uk/Museums/Documents/ policy%20documents/Note%20on%20return%20of%20I ndigenous%20Australian%20Human%20Remains.doc

Native American Graves Protection and Repatriation Act
www.nps.gov/nagpra/

www.nps.gov/history/nagpra/mandates/25USC3001etseq.htm

Professional bodies

Information and Records Management Society
www.irms.org.uk/

Archives and Records Association
www.archives.org.uk

Society of American Archivists Museum Archives Section
www.archivists.org./saagroups/museum/

Discussion lists

Archivists, conservators and records managers
https://www.jiscmail.ac.uk/cgi-bin/webadmin?A0=archives-nra

Museum Information and Records Management listserv
*https://www.jiscmail.ac.uk/cgi-bin/webadmin?AO=MU
SEUMINFO-RECORDS*

Useful guidance and training

Glossary of records management terms
www.ucl.ac.uk/~uczcw09/appraisl/characs.html

*https://www.nationalarchives.gov.uk/documents/whatisa
publicrecord.pdf*

Information Commissioner's Office
www.dataprotection.gov.uk

Information Commissioner's Office Register of Data Controllers
www.ico.gov.uk/ESDaWebPages/search.asp

Local Government Classification Scheme
http://doc.esd.org.uk/ClassificationList/3.00.html

Records storage
www.nationalarchives.gov.uk/documents/considerations-for-developing-an-offsite-store.pdf

www.nationalarchives.gov.uk/documents/stan_semicurrent.pdf
http://shop.bsigroup.com/en/ProductDetail/?pid=00000000 0019996363

Renaissance London Information and Records Management project guidance and training materials

- Information and records management network and training
www.collectionslink.org.uk

www.museumoflondon.org.uk/Corporate/About-us/Regional-Programmes/Regional+projects.htm

- Data protection e-learning tool
www.museuminfo-records.org.uk/resources/DPAe-tool/

- Museum information policy toolkit
www.museuminfo-records.org.uk/toolkits/Information Policy.pdf

- Museum information management e-learning tool
www.museuminfo-records.org.uk/resources/IMe-tool/

- Museum records management e-learning tool
www.museuminfo-records.org.uk/resources/RMe-tool/

- Museum records management toolkit
www.museuminfo-records.org.uk/toolkits/Records Management.pdf

TNA Advisory Services provide guidance on all aspects of archive and records management, including electronic records and Data Protection Act compliance
www.nationalarchives.gov.uk/information-management/ our-services.htm

www.nationalarchives.gov.uk/documents/dp-code-of-practice.pdf

TNA Archives Inspection Unit
https://www.nationalarchives.gov.uk/documents/whatisapublic record.pdf

www.nationalarchives.gov.uk/documents/inspectionsleaflet.pdf

Standards

British Standards Institute (for information about and purchase of ISO 15489, BS 10008, BS 5454, BS PD0025-2, etc.)
www.bsigroup.co.uk/

ISAD(G)
www.icacds.org.uk/eng/ISAD(G).pdf

Museum Archives Guidelines
www.archivists.org/governance/guidelines/museum_ guidelines.asp

SPECTRUM
www.collectionslink.org.uk/manage-information/spectrum

Bibliography

Callister, Tim and Blake, Richard (2009) *Identifying and Specifying Requirements for Offsite Storage of Physical Records.* London: TNA.

Cook, Michael and Proctor, Margaret (2000) *Manual of Archival Description*, 3rd edn. Aldershot: Gower Publishing.

NPO Preservation Guidance (2003) *Basic Preservation Guidelines for Library and Archive Collections*, Preservation in Practice Series. London: British Library.

The National Archives (1999) *Routemap and Milestones for Electronic Records Management by 2004*. London: TNA.

Appendix 1:
Risk assessment template and scoring framework

Information/records management risk register

Division/function/project: **Information management** Completed by: **Head, department** Date completed: Updated: **month, year**

Objectives: To manage organisational information risk

The risk What can happen? The source How can it happen?	Current controls and their effectiveness E = Effective P = Partially effective I = Ineffective		Actual risk rating			Treatments What are we going to do to mitigate this risk further?	Residual risk rating			Treatment completion date And/or **Date of next review**	Risk owner (Name and job title)
			Likelihood	Impact	Risk (colour)		Likelihood	Impact	Risk		
1. Lack of comprehensive oversight and control • Lack of understanding regarding data privacy issues	FOIA/DPA induction training implemented	P				Review compliance with specific legislation (e.g. DPA)					
	Records management policy	E				Roll out DPA training as part of mandatory induction and provide refresher training on demand or as needed				June 2010	Records manager
	Training on museum records management	P								June 2010	Records manager
	Data protection policy and procedures implemented	P				Use all-staff briefings to flag guidance and other resources				Ongoing	Head and records manager

The risk — What can happen? The source. How can it happen?	Current controls and their effectiveness — E = Effective, P = Partially effective, I = Ineffective	Actual risk rating — Likelihood	Impact	Risk (colour)	Treatments — What are we going to do to mitigate this risk further?	Residual risk rating — Likelihood	Impact	Risk	Treatment completion date And/or Date of next review	Risk owner (Name and job title)
2. Critical information and records are wrongly destroyed, not kept, duplicated or cannot be found when needed					Full-time records manager in post				Ongoing	Records manager
• Staff are not clear on what information needs to be kept, where or for how long	Records management, FOIA/EIR and DPA policies, information management policy in place — E				Corporate file plan implemented				July 2010	Records manager
• Relevant legislation is not understood or correctly followed					Departmental retention schedules implemented				November 2010	Records manager
	Information and records management strategy — E				Records store identified				2010	Records manager
• Systems are unable to support the retention of corporate information					Compliance audits conducted				May 2010	Records manager
• Policies and procedures relating to the management of information are not followed correctly	E-learning tools on records management, DPA and information management — P				Guidance to staff on what should be placed in the intranet versus the shared drive				June 2010	Records manager
	Standard operating procedures for back-up — P				Implement guidance on e-mail management				July 2010	Records manager
					Embed compliance with records and information policies into PMD [performance management and development] process as a staff-wide objective where appropriate (to Information Committee?)				July 2011	Human resources with records manager
					Back-ups policy (including disposal schedule)				Late 2010	IT with records manager

The risk *What can happen?* **The source** *How can it happen?*	Current controls *and their effectiveness* E = Effective P = Partially effective I = Ineffective	Actual risk rating			Treatments *What are we going to do to mitigate this risk further?*	Residual risk rating			Treatment completion date And/or Date of next review	Risk owner (Name and job title)
		Likelihood	Impact	Risk (colour)		Likelihood	Impact	Risk		
3. Critical information is lost (with legal, reputational or financial consequences) due to major disasters, incidents or poor environmental control of stores										
• Business continuity plans do not identify key information required to run the business with appropriate backup strategies	IT risk register E Current back-up strategy P				Robust back-up strategy for electronic records mirrored at separate locations				2011	IT with records manager
• Business records of permanent value to the museum are not maintained and accessible at industry-standard levels	Temporary partial storage I				Records store planned and agreed Regular transfers of archival materials are made to permanent store				July 2010 Ongoing once store in place	Records manager Records manager
4. Despite having procedures and rules, staff, acting in error, do the wrong thing (and consequences occur)										
• Information not valued as an asset by the organisation • Information risk not seen as important as other risks • Information procedures not in place or not understood • Information procedures/polices not enforced • Information management not linked to performance management	Records management, DPA and FOIA policies and procedures embedded into induction Records management e-learning tool FOIA lead users for each department or division				Information policy Information map Key systems, such as collections management, human resources and finance databases, have audit logs switched on and monitored				2010 2010 2010	Department head Department head Selected departments with IT and records manager

The risk What can happen? The source How can it happen?	Current controls and their effectiveness E = Effective P = Partially effective I = Ineffective	Actual risk rating			Treatments What are we going to do to mitigate this risk further?	Residual risk rating			Treatment completion date And/or Date of next review	Risk owner (Name and job title)
		Likelihood	Impact	Risk (colour)		Likelihood	Impact	Risk		
• Key data access lacks control and is difficult to audit • Staff are unclear about the responsibilities for information management within the organisation	Lead users list disseminated FOIA consult list disseminated Departmental training implemented				Key systems have dedicated systems administrators responsible for monitoring permissions and access (lead users list)				2011/12?	Human resources with department head
					Embed information management into the performance management process				2010	Head and records manager
					Information management e-learning tool deployed				2011	Head
					Guidance for staff about information sharing				Sept 2010	IT
					FOIA lead users list				Late 2010	AM, IT
					IT security policies				2010/11	Security committee
5. External parties obtain information illegally (and expose it, act maliciously or defraud museum and/or customers) • Records are disposed of incorrectly/insecurely	Records management training in place Secure shredding service				Records management retention guidance on shredding and secure disposal implemented				2010	Records manager

The risk What can happen? The source How can it happen?	Current controls and their effectiveness E = Effective P = Partially effective I = Ineffective	Actual risk rating			Treatments What are we going to do to mitigate this risk further?	Residual risk rating			Treatment completion date And/or Date of next review	Risk owner (Name and job title)
		Likelihood	Impact	Risk (colour)		Likelihood	Impact	Risk		
6. Failure to disclose critical information correctly (causing reputational damage or worse) • Staff do not correctly understand the relevant legislation	FOIA/EIR and DPA policy, procedures and guidelines for staff Records management e-learning tool (which includes FOIA) FOIA lead users in each department				DPA e-learning tool Staff refresher training				July 2010 Bi-annually	Records manager Records manager
7. Failure to utilise the value of the information asset (leading to a waste of public money) • Inappropriate or inadequate use of the publication scheme • Inadequate or incomplete logging of information requests	Annual review of publication scheme Departmental logs Central FOIA log of cross-departmental enquiries				Incorporating frequently answered queries regularly into the FAQ on the website Annual review of departmental logs?				Quarterly Annually	Records manager Records manager

Risk rating

Likelihood	Criteria used to establish rating
A. Almost certain	The risk event will occur in most circumstances.
B. Likely	The event will probably occur at least once.
C. Possible	The event might occur at some time.
D. Unlikely	The event is not expected to occur.
E. Rare	The probability of the event occurring is negligible.

	Impact (consequence)				
	How severe could the impact be if the risk event occurs?				
Likelihood (probability) — What's the chance of the risk occurring?	5. Insignificant	4. Minor	3. Moderate	2. Major	1. Severe
A. Almost certain	Medium	Medium	High	High	Extreme
B. Likely	Low	Medium	Medium	High	High
C. Possible	Low	Low	Medium	Medium	High
D. Unlikely	Negligible	Low	Low	Medium	Medium
E. Rare	Negligible	Negligible	Low	Low	Medium

Source: By kind permission of the Museum of London.

Appendix 2:
Business case example

1. Introduction

Implementing a records management programme will not only benefit the museum by securing regulatory compliance, it will also help safeguard vital information; protect against litigation; preserve the historical memory of the organisation; and secure economies of time and space.

2. Defining the boundaries of the records management programme

2.1 Approach

In line with functional appraisal, the records life cycle, and the provisions of the Freedom of Information Act, the records management programme will take a holistic approach to the museum's records, taking into consideration all of its records, across all departments, in all formats, from the foundation of the museum to the present day.

The records management programme will focus on the museum's more recent records (those currently being created, stored in departments and more recently transferred to the archive), but the guidelines and recommendations made will be informed by, and will benefit, the whole.

2.2 Definitions and terminology

All records created by the museum – regardless of age or format – are public records.

Records are documents in any format that have been generated or received by the museum in the course of its activities and have been, or may be, used by the museum as evidence of its actions and decisions, or because of their information content. This does not include works in the object collections. Records can be held in any format including paper documents, photographs, e-mails, videos, slides, audio recordings, databases or any multimedia formats.

Records management is the strategic and systematic control of the creation, receipt, maintenance, use and disposal or preservation or records.

Archive records are records that have been subject to a qualitative assessment, have been identified as having continuing value either for the institution or the public and thus have been marked for permanent preservation.

The museum's records represent an extremely valuable resource, as they document the main concerns, functions, working practices and history of the institution itself. The appraisal procedure should recognise this value, and the archive be developed and promoted to reflect this.

The collected archives owned by – rather than deposited in – the museum are subject to the provisions of the Freedom of Information Act and must be managed accordingly.

3. Establishing the record-keeping situation at the museum

3.1 Record-keeping history

Due to both the size of the institution and the fact that records have long been recognised as a valuable research tool, the museum's records have been relatively well maintained, with the majority of records – at least in the early years – filed into three main series.

3.2 Current record-keeping situation

Since the expansion of the museum and the development of electronic records, record-keeping practices have become less consistent in recent years and now vary from department to department. As a result, some of the museum's activities are not documented in the archive at all, and others contain a huge amount of duplication.

4. Implementing the records management programme

4.1 Aims and objectives

The first stage in introducing a records management programme is to conduct a record survey. This is an information-gathering exercise which aims to collect as much information as possible about the institution's records.

Records management is an ongoing activity which must be reviewed and developed on a continuing basis in line with internal and external developments.

4.2 Records management policy

A vital component of a records management programme is the records management policy: this document is a necessary requirement under the Freedom of Information Act, 2000, and should define the gallery's record-keeping commitment and responsibilities.

4.3 Forward planning

It is estimated that it will take one year to complete the record survey. Work will be led by the records manager, but will involve staff from across the museum. Key records management documents – retention schedule, appraisal procedure, supporting policies and guidance – will be developed in the second year.

Author: Charlotte Brunskill.
Source: By kind permission of the National Portrait Gallery.

Appendix 3:
Sample data protection survey form

Department name ....

Post title ....

Surveyor name ....

Date ....

1. Name of the record series/ type containing personal data	E.g. Membership records
2. Post/s responsible for record series identified	E.g. Membership officer
3. In what format does the record series/type exist?	Paper Electronic/digital
4. If in paper format, does it exist as part of a relevant filing system?	Yes No

5. Where did the personal data contained in these records originally come from?	Collected via (please list all sources): E.g. Membership application forms
6. When the personal data were collected did the individual see a data protection statement (i.e. was a data protection statement included on the original collection form)?	Yes No
7. In the first instance, the personal data contained within these records are used/processed in the following ways	To administer a booking/ application/donation/ order Other (please give details)
8. The personal data are subsequently used/processed in the following ways (please tick any boxes that apply)	To send details of museum activities, services, events, publications, gifts, special offers, fundraising activities, etc. To send information about other carefully selected appropriate parties To send the museum's e-newsletter Other (please give details)

9. The personal data are subsequently passed to the following third parties	Similar cultural and heritage organisations (e.g. museums/galleries/ heritage institutions) Other (please give details)
10. The personal data contained in this record series are used/processed by the following groups	This department only Other museum departments (please give details) External bodies (please give details)
11. Are the personal data transferred outside the EEA?	Yes (if so, where?) No

Author: Charlotte Brunskill.
Source: By kind permission of the National Portrait Gallery.

Appendix 4:
Museum record series commonly containing personal data

Collections management, curatorial and directorate

- Object files (all collections)
- Offers register
- Offers files
- Proposed bequest files (see also Development)
- Accessions registers
- Accessions files
- Collections database
- Director's correspondence, A–Z
- Research correspondence, A–Z
- General enquiries, A–Z

Exhibitions

- Exhibition lenders files
- Exhibition loan database
- Exhibition case files

- Exhibition proposals declined
- Exhibition proposals database

Information desk/research office/visitor services

- Visitor agreement forms
- Visitor enquiries
- Visitor books
- Visitor comments forms/cards
- Visitor comments database
- Desk diaries

Development

- Individual member records
- Individual patron records
- Membership scheme, weekly financial records
- Patrons scheme, income files
- Membership scheme questionnaires
- Requests for legacy information
- Membership questionnaires database
- Development database
- Development/supporters files, arranged by name

Education

- Education workshop case files
- School visits case files
- Booking forms
- Booking database
- Gallery talks/lectures attendance lists

- Education activities attendance database or spreadsheets
- Conferences and study days database
- Photographs of individuals (including children)
- Freelancer CVs

Health and safety

- Individual workstation assessments (occupational health and safety)
- List of first aiders
- Accident/incident reports

Personnel/human resources

- Personnel case files (including application forms, details of sick leave, holidays, annual reviews, disciplinary hearings, etc.)
- Speculative and unsuccessful application forms and CVs
- Staff lists and contact details
- Training database

Picture library

- Copyright permissions files
- Copyright database
- Picture library orders, completed and outstanding
- Licences
- Contracts (with suppliers, photographers, etc.)
- Agency agreements (external items)
- Agency statements
- Picture library database

Publications and trading

- Contracts records
- Royalties records
- Contact details
- Shop orders and payments including credit card details

Buildings

- Permits to work
- CCTV footage

Finance

- Payroll database

IT

- Permissions database (including passwords)

Author: Charlotte Brunskill.
Source: By kind permission of the National Portrait Gallery.

Appendix 5:
Sample data protection policies

The National Portrait Gallery Data Protection Policy

1. Introduction

The National Portrait Gallery needs to keep certain personal data, for example about staff, visitors, sitters and artists, in order to fulfil its purpose. Under the provisions of the Data Protection Act 1998, which came into force on 1 March 2000, the Gallery has a legal duty to ensure that this personal information is collected and used fairly, stored safely and not disclosed to any other person or organisation unlawfully. The purpose of the Act is 'to protect the fundamental rights and freedoms of natural persons, in particular their right to privacy' and in doing so it also provides data subjects (i.e. individuals about whom personal information is processed) increased protection through express new rights. The policy can be found on the staff network at xxxxxxxxxx

2. Scope

The aim of this policy is both to ensure that all staff are aware of their particular responsibilities in relation to the Data Protection Act and its associated Codes of Practice; and to inform members of the public how the Gallery complies with the legislation. It is also to minimise the risk of the Gallery breaching the Act; thereby potentially damaging valued relationships with staff; customers; and other audiences as well as its reputation.

This policy covers all *personal data* held in *electronic* format or in *relevant manual filing systems*, that is *processed* by the National Portrait Gallery. (For definitions: see below.)

It applies to all individuals working for the National Portrait Gallery in whatever role. This includes permanent and contracted Gallery staff, as well as temporary employees; volunteers; interns etc.

3. Definitions

Under the terms of the Act:

- *Personal data* means information about a living person who can be identified from that information.
- *Data subject* means the individual about whom the personal data is held.
- *Processing* means obtaining, holding, organising, retrieving, altering etc. In fact virtually any activity concerned with the data.
- *Electronic* format means data held as Word documents; e-mails; in databases etc.

- *Relevant manual filing systems* means a filing system in which information about individuals is readily available. For example: files ordered alphabetically by name (exhibition lenders files; staff files; icon notes); or by which there is another point of access (reference number system etc.). It does *not* apply to incidental references to individuals in files structured by reference to topics not relating to those individuals.

4. Legal basis

The Data Protection Act 1998.

5. Statement of principles

The National Portrait Gallery is committed to the eight *Data Protection Principles* contained in the Data Protection Act 1998. These represent the minimum standards of practice for any organisation with respect to personal data and state that it must be:

1. processed *fairly and lawfully*;
2. obtained only for the *purposes specified* and shall only be processed for those purposes;
3. *adequate, relevant and not excessive* for the purpose for which they are processed;
4. *accurate and kept up to date*;
5. *kept for no longer than is necessary*;
6. processed in accordance with the *rights of data subjects* under the 1998 Data Protection Act;

7. protected against *unauthorised processing* of personal data and against accidental loss or destruction to personal data;

8 *not transferred outside the European Economic Area* without adequate protection.

Rights of data subjects

- Any individual data subject, including staff, has the right to ask what information the National Portrait Gallery holds about them and why this is being held.

- If any such information is held, an individual data subject also has the right, on request:

  a) to see any personal data that is being kept about them on computer, and also to have access to paper based data held in relevant manual filing systems

  b) to be informed as to how to get the information updated or amended

  c) to be informed as to any regular or possible recipients of the information.

- Any person who wishes to exercise this right should make the request in writing to the Data Protection Officer. *If an access request is received by any other members of staff it should be forwarded to the Data Protection Officer.*

- The National Portrait Gallery will comply with requests for access to personal information as quickly as possible. In compliance with the law, this will always be within 40 calendar days of receipt of a request.

- As well as right of subject access, individual data subjects have the right to object to direct marketing, including marketing of the National Portrait Gallery's products and services. Where an individual decides to exercise this right, this fact should be accurately recorded.

- As well as a right of subject access, individual data subjects may, in certain circumstances, have other rights under the Act, including the right to have inaccurate information corrected. The Data Protection Officer should be informed if a request to exercise this right is received.

6. Responsibilities

- The *Board of Trustees* of the National Portrait Gallery is the *Data Controller* – the Data Controller is the legal entity who must comply with the Act and ensure that its provisions are upheld in all processing across the Gallery.

- The *Head of Administration* is the Gallery's *Data Protection Officer*. The Data Protection Officer is accountable and responsible for overseeing all Data Protection activities and promoting compliance throughout the Gallery. Under the terms of the Act, the National Portrait Gallery is obliged to prepare an annual notification to the Information Commissioner providing details of the types of data it processes and for what purpose. The Data Protection Officer is the individual responsible for ensuring that the Gallery's entry is complete and up to date (assistance will be provided by the Records Manager). The current register entry can be found through the Information Commissioner's website.

- The *Records Manager* will act as the first point of contact for Data Protection queries throughout the Gallery; make suggestions for best practice; and identify areas of risk. The Records Manager will work with identified liaison staff and Heads of Department to promote compliance within departments but it is the responsibility of Heads of Department to address any risks identified and to ensure that the provisions of the Act are upheld (see below). The Records Manager has specific responsibility for determining retention periods for records and ensuring that the Gallery's Register of Records caught by the Act is accurate and up to date.

- *Heads of Departments* will be accountable for Data Protection compliance in their departments. It is their responsibility to ensure that all processing within their area complies with the Act, in particular that all points of personal data collection include Data Protection statements; that any contracts or agreements with external contractors processing personal data on the Gallery's behalf (e.g. distribution or mailing services; data converters etc.) include a relevant Data Protection clause; that risks are identified and managed appropriately; that staff receive adequate training; and that legal advice is sought where necessary. Their responsibilities also include following Best Practice documents where applicable; as well as supporting the work of the identified liaison staff in their area.

- *Identified liaison staff* will be responsible for overseeing the practical application of the Data Protection Act in their department/area. It is their responsibility to communicate basic information about the Act to their department; and raise any concerns about how the department collects and manages personal data with their Head of Department. They must also ensure that the Records Manager is informed of any changes to data processing in their areas, so that the Gallery's Register of Records caught by the Act can be amended accordingly. Their role is to provide the first point of contact between the Records Manager and the department and as such they must ensure they have a basic understanding of the Act – this includes attending Data Protection training sessions or liaison group meetings as and when required.

- The *Personnel Department*, in conjunction with the Records Manager, will ensure that appropriate guidance and training on compliance with the Data Protection Act 1998 is made available to all staff engaged in the processing of personal data.

- *All Gallery staff* who process personal information in the course of their work will be responsible for ensuring compliance with the legislation and this policy document. The Gallery will ensure that staff are given appropriate training to fulfil this responsibility

- *All external data processors* processing personal data on behalf of the National Portrait Gallery (i.e. third parties) are contractually required to comply with the Data Protection Act 1998 and any associated Codes of Practice. Heads of Department are responsible for ensuring that this is upheld (see above).

7. Procedures

The Gallery will organise an annual training session for liaison staff.

Additional best practice procedure will be available on the staff network drive.

A set of model Data Protection statements (approved by the Gallery's external legal advisers) can found in Appendix 1.

8. Breach

Breach of data protection legislation is a criminal offence and the National Portrait Gallery will regard wilful or reckless breach of this data protection policy as a disciplinary offence and such breaches will be subject to the Gallery's disciplinary procedures.

9. Review

This policy will be reviewed every 5 years.

Next review: April 2011.

10. Date of approval

Approved at the 724th meeting of the Trustees on 18/05/2006.

Author: Charlotte Brunskill.
Source: By kind permission of the National Portrait Gallery.

Museum of London Data Protection Policy

1. Introduction

This document sets out the Museum of London's policy regarding the handling of personal data, as defined by the Data Protection Act 1998. It specifies the framework which the Museum uses to manage compliance with the requirements of the Act. It outlines the steps that are taken to ensure this compliance and identifies the responsibilities of staff at the various levels of the organisation.

2. Scope

This policy applies to all personal data held by the Museum, whether in manual or electronic systems, which provides access to information relating to a specific individual. This includes information in the form of CCTV footage.

The policy applies to the Museum and the Archaeological Services and all references to the Museum include these services.

3. Purpose

- To ensure the security and proper handling of personal data as defined by the Act;
- To uphold the rights of data subjects;

- To ensure the application of the 8 Data Protection Principles (see Appendix 1);

- To ensure that notification to the Information Commissioner is kept up to date, and that it continues to reflect the Museum's data protection policies and procedures;

- To ensure all staff are aware of the Museum's obligations under the Act and their role in supporting this;

- To define what personal data the Museum holds and how this will be safeguarded.

4. Definition of terms

4.1 *Data Controller* – A person or named organisation, who determines the purpose for which and the manner in which any personal data are, or will be, processed. (The Museum of London is the Data Controller for the purposes of notification.)

4.2 *Data Subject* – An individual about whom personal data is held.

4.3 *Notification* – The process by which a data controller's details are added to the register (maintained by the Information Commissioner).

4.4 *Personal Data* – Information from which a living person can be identified.

4.5 *Sensitive Information* – Data relating to a person's:

- racial or ethnic origin
- political opinions
- religious or other beliefs of a similar nature

- trade union membership
- physical or mental health or condition
- sexual life
- offences (including alleged offences)
- criminal proceedings, outcomes and sentence.

5. Responsibilities

5.1 Directorate

The Director will appoint a Data Protection Officer to oversee compliance with the Act.

5.2 Data Protection Officer

The Head of Information Resources (IRS) is the Data Protection Officer for the Museum and is responsible for overseeing compliance with the Act by the following measures:

a) Ensuring that the Museum's registration with the Information Commissioner is kept up to date

b) Advising Senior Management, departments and staff about Data Protection issues

c) Writing any guidelines, procedures and related documentation for compliance with the Act, including this policy

d) Coordinating the Museum's response to requests from members of the public and museum staff for access to records relating to them, correction of such data, etc.

e) Investigating any apparent breach of data security and informing the Executive Committee.

3.3 Records Manager

The Records Manager is responsible for the practical implementation of the above compliance measures with the exception of (e), which is the sole responsibility of the Data Protection Officer.

3.4 Managers

Individual managers are responsible for ensuring that their staff comply with this policy and the related procedures. If local procedures are required, managers are to draw up and issue written procedures in consultation with the Data Protection Officer. Managers are also responsible for notifying the Data Protection Officer of any new personal data they (or their staff) intend to collect if it is different from the purposes listed in Appendix 2.

5.4 Employees

Compliance with the Act is a requirement for all employees, and all staff must ensure that they read and then follow the Museum policy (this document) and the procedures and guidelines. Additionally, all staff are responsible for ensuring that any personal information they hold about other people is kept securely and is not disclosed in any form to any unauthorised third party.

5.5 Human Resources

Human Resources, in conjunction with IRS, will ensure that Data Protection training is included as part of induction for new staff and that ongoing training is also available.

6. Policy

6.1 The Museum will comply with the data protection principles as set out in the Act.

6.2 The Museum will monitor compliance with the Data Protection Act by auditing its notification every three years, starting in August 2008. The Museum's notification will be amended to take account of any changes identified by this audit.

6.3 The Museum will ensure that its procedures relating to the holding, use and disclosure of personal data are in accordance with the notification.

6.4 The Museum will ensure the notification is kept up to date, so that it continues to reflect the Museum's data protection policies and procedures.

6.5 The Museum observes the rights of data subjects to have access to their personal data held and processed by the Museum (subject to the qualifications provided for in the Act).

6.6 The Museum will ensure all such data is accurate and not processed unnecessarily.

6.7 Written requests for information will receive a response within 40 calendar days. The Museum reserves the right to charge a fee of £10 for fulfilling such requests.

6.8 The Museum will investigate any identified breach of data security and take appropriate action.

6.9 The Museum will take appropriate steps to protect personal data from loss and unauthorised access and will review arrangements regularly.

6.10 Data will be collected and processed only for specified purposes listed in the Notification (Appendix 2) and will only be viewed by those who need to see it.

6.11 Where someone is required to provide personal information to the Museum they will be informed of the reason(s) for its collection, and given the opportunity to agree to its use for other purposes, such as news of future events arranged by the Museum.

7. Guidance on supporting procedures, related policies and the regulatory environment

7.1 This policy is related to the *Freedom of Information Policy* and *Interim Records Management policy*.

8. Queries

8.1 If you have any questions about this policy, please contact the Head of Information Resources.

Appendix 1: Principles

The 8 data protection principles set out in the Act require that data be:

- fairly and lawfully processed
- processed for limited purposes
- adequate, relevant and not excessive in relation to the purpose for which it is held
- accurate and up to date
- not kept longer than necessary for the purpose for which it was originally processed
- processed in accordance with the data subjects' rights

- secure against unauthorised or unlawful processing, loss, destruction or damage

- not transferred to countries outside the European Economic Area without adequate protection.

Appendix 2: Purposes

The Museum holds personal information in central and local computer systems and manual systems. The Museum has identified the 'purposes' (reasons why) for which it holds personal data, the sources of this data and the use made of the data.

The purposes are:

- Accounts and finance records
- Administration of membership records
- Advertising, marketing and public relations
- Advertising, marketing and public relations for others (e.g. London Museums Hub)
- Consultancy and advisory services
- Crime prevention and prosecution of offenders
- Education
- Fundraising
- Information and databank administration
- Journalism and media
- Pensions administration
- Records selected as archives, for historic and other research
- Research
- Staff administration and recruitment.

Notes:

Personal information and historical research/collections management

Records which are processed only for historical research purposes and the operation of certain collections management procedures (such as acquisition) may be kept indefinitely and therefore are exempt from the fifth data protection principle.

[Reviewed every three years.]

Source: By kind permission of the Museum of London.

Appendix 6:
Sample data protection statements

Introduction

Under the terms of the Data Protection Act, the museum is obliged to supply the following information at all instances where it requests personal data. This includes personal data collected in hard-copy format (i.e. paper form), or electronically (i.e. via e-mail or the website).

1. The name of the Data Controller, i.e. the XXXX museum.
2. The purpose for which the personal data are being collected (e.g. administering a booking, answering an enquiry etc.).
3. Clear contact details for the museum (somewhere on the form, if not necessarily part of the statement itself).
4. Details about any further ways in which the museum would like to use the personal data (in particular, marketing or promotional purposes), together with an opt-in box requesting permission to do so.
5. A statement about the means by which the museum will contact the data subject if permission is given for the data to be used for direct marketing (this includes marketing of the museum's own products and services).

Instructions

The Data Protection Statement should be situated immediately below the part of the form where the personal data are being requested and should be clearly visible.

It is the responsibility of department heads to ensure that any personal data collected in their area contain an appropriate Data Protection Statement. The following standard statements have been prepared to assist with this and have been approved by the museum's external legal advisers. Where the text is in italics you should include only if relevant.

Standard statements

1. Standard statement – compulsory on all forms.

Data Protection

XXXX museum is committed to protecting your privacy. All personal data given on this form will be held securely by XXXX and (unless you agree otherwise) only be used to administer your *[booking/application/order/ donation etc.]*. They will not be passed to any third parties unless you agree.

---

2. Additional optional statements.

2.1 To be included if you or another museum department would like to use the personal data for marketing, or promoting other museum activities or events.

From time to time, we would also like to inform you by post, phone and e-mail about additional museum [*activities, services, events, publications, gifts, special offers, fundraising activities etc.*] that may be of interest.

☐ Yes, I would like to receive this information.

2.2 To be included if you would like to send data subjects information from other institutions (NB. This does not cover disclosing the personal data to other third-party institutions for them to market their events, etc. – in such cases, use the wording in 2.3 below.)

Occasionally, we may also like to inform you by post, phone and e-mail of [*events, news and special offers*] from other carefully selected appropriate parties.

☐ Yes, I would like to receive this information.

2.3 To be included if you would like to pass personal details on to a third party (NB. The third party/parties selected must fit the description of 'similar cultural and heritage organisations' otherwise this will not comply with the legal requirements.)

Occasionally we would like to pass your data to similar cultural and heritage organisation third parties so that they can send you information by post, phone and e-mail about [*events, news and special offers*].

☐ Yes, I would like to receive this information.

2.4 To be included if you would like to send data subjects the e-newsletter.

We would like to inform you about the exhibitions, collections and activities of the museum via e-mail. Our monthly e-newsletter contains advance information about events, museum news, special offers and exclusive competitions.

☐ Yes, I would like to receive the e-newsletter.

---

3. Statements for education workshops involving photographs of students.

Data Protection

XXXX museum is committed to protecting your privacy. All personal data given on this form will be held securely by the museum and (unless you agree otherwise) only be used to administer your [booking/application/order/ donation etc.]. They will not be passed to any third parties unless you agree.

Please be advised that as part of standard workshop activity museum staff may take some photographs of participants. We may, in some cases, use these images to publicise the museum's services (on the website, in promotional leaflets, displays etc.). They may also be retained permanently for historical research purposes.

☐ I give permission for my image to be taken and used in this way.

☐ I give permission for images of .... to be taken and used in this way (parent/guardian if under 18)

---

4. For patron/membership applications.

Data Protection

XXXX museum is committed to protecting your privacy. All personal data given on this form will be held securely. They will be used to administer your *[patron/ membership application]* and thereafter to provide you with information about events, benefits, services and special offers available to donors. They will not be passed to any third parties unless you agree.

From time to time we may also wish to contact you about XXXX museum's fundraising programmes.

☐ Yes, I would like to receive this information.

Occasionally we would like to send you information of events, news and special offers from other carefully selected appropriate parties.

☐ Yes, I would like to receive this information.

NB. The wording by the second tick box does not permit disclosure of information to third parties.

5. For job application forms (Personnel).

Data Protection

XXXX museum is committed to protecting your privacy. All personal data provided on this form will be held securely and used in the first instance only to administer the recruitment process. They will not be passed to any third parties.

Once the recruitment process is complete the application forms of successful candidates will be retained and will form the basis of the personnel records. Information provided on the Equal Opportunities

---

Monitoring Form will be used to monitor the museum's equal opportunities policy and practices.

By signing and submitting your completed application form you are consenting to your personal data being managed as above (if you submit your application by e-mail and the form is unsigned we will assume that consent is given by you).

Personal data relating to unsuccessful candidates will be stored for a maximum of 6 months and then destroyed.

Source: By kind permission of the National Portrait Gallery.

Appendix 7:
Data subject access request form

Museum of London Data Subject Access Request Form

Are you a member or former member of staff?   Yes/no

---

1 Details of person requesting the information

Full name

Address

Postcode

Tel. No.   Fax No.

E-mail address

---

2 Are you the data subject?

Yes. If you are the data subject please supply evidence of your identity, i.e. driving licence, passport, national identity card or photo-pass, and a recent letter or bill from a utility company as evidence of address. Original documents should be sent by recorded delivery and will be retuned to you. Please provide a self-addressed envelope for the return of the documents. *(Please go to question 4.)*

No. Are you acting on behalf of the data subject with their written authority? If so, that authority must be enclosed. If not, what other legal justification have you for obtaining access to the data? (Note that appropriate identification as above must also be provided.) *(Please go to question 3.)*

Please note that the Museum may request further information to verify your identity after receipt of the information listed above.

---

3 Details of the data subject (if different from 1)

Full name

Address

Tel. No.   Fax No.

E-mail address

Please describe your relationship with the data subject that leads you to make this request for information on their behalf.

4 Please describe the information you seek together with any other relevant information. This will help to identify the information you require. If you are requesting CCTV images from a visit to us please specify the date of your visit and the site you visited.

We are allowed charge a fee of £10 for each application: an invoice will be forwarded to you and must be paid before we will proceed with your enquiry.

DECLARATION. To be completed by all applicants. Please note that any attempt to mislead may result in prosecution.

I .... certify that the information given on this application form to the Museum of London is true. I understand that it is necessary for the Museum of London to confirm my/the data subject's identity and it may be necessary to obtain more detailed information in order to locate the correct personal data.

Signature: Date:

Note. The period of 40 days in which the Museum of London must respond to the request will not begin until it is satisfied on these matters.

Please return the completed form to:
The Data Protection Co-ordinator
Information Resources Section
Museum of London
London Wall
London
EC2Y 5HN

Documents which must accompany this application:
- evidence of your identity

- evidence of the data subject's identity (if different from above)

- authorisation from the data subject to act on their behalf (if applicable)

- a self-addressed envelope for return of proof of identity/authority documents.

Source: By kind permission of the Museum of London.

Appendix 8:
Sample records management policy

National Portrait Gallery Archives and Records Management Policy

1. Introduction

The National Portrait Gallery recognises that its records are an essential business resource; and that their efficient management is necessary to support its core functions, to comply with its legal and regulatory obligations and to contribute to the effective overall management of the institution. This paper sets out the policy with regard to all records created and managed by the Gallery as part of its everyday business. This policy document can be found on the staff network at: xxxx

2. Scope

The aim of this policy is to provide a framework for managing the Gallery's records; to support the development of a Records Management programme; and thereby to minimise the risk of breach of relevant legislation (see 4. Legal basis).

This policy applies to all records created, received and maintained by the staff and employees of the National Portrait Gallery in the course of their work.

3. Definitions

A *record* is a document in any format that has been generated or received by the National Portrait Gallery in the course of its activities and has been, or may be, used by the Gallery as evidence of its actions and decisions, or because of its information content. This does not include works in the primary, photographs, reference or library collections. Records can be held in any format including paper documents, photographs, e-mails, videos, slides, audio recordings, databases or any multimedia formats.

Records Management is the strategic and systematic control of the creation, receipt, maintenance, use and disposal or preservation or records.

Archives are records selected for permanent preservation as part of the Gallery's corporate memory, and as a resource for research.

4. Legal basis

The records of the National Portrait Gallery are subject to, and therefore will be managed in accordance with, the following legislation:

- The Public Records Acts, 1958 and 1967
- The Museums and Galleries Act, 1992
- The Data Protection Act, 1998
- The Freedom of Information Act, 2000
- The Requirements of HM Customs & Revenue

As part of the Records Management programme, the Gallery is also working towards the Modernising Government Agenda, which states that all newly created public records should be stored and retrieved electronically.

Until issues relating to the management and long-term preservation of electronic records have been addressed, the current policy is for significant electronic records to be printed and stored in paper files wherever possible: this will be reviewed in 2010.

5. Statement of principles

General

- The National Portrait Gallery is committed to creating, keeping and managing its records in a manner that accurately documents its principal activities.

- It is committed to a culture of openness and access to information wherever possible, in accordance with statutory requirements.

- It fully supports a centralised and Gallery-wide Records Management programme that is based on national and international standards in the field (e.g. BSI ISO 15489:2001).

Ownership of records

- All records created and received by the National Portrait Gallery in the course of its business are owned by the National Portrait Gallery, and not by the individuals, departments or teams that create the records.

- Records must not be removed from the offices of the National Portrait Gallery or used for any activity or purpose other than the Gallery's official business.

Purpose of records management

Records Management will help ensure that the Gallery:

- Achieves its objectives to promote through the medium of portraits the appreciation and understanding of the men and women who have made and are making British history and culture; and to promote the understanding and appreciation of portraiture in all media.

- Creates and captures authentic and reliable records to demonstrate evidence, accountability and information about its decisions, activities and collections.

- Maintains securely, and preserves access to, those records as long as they are required to support Gallery operations, including audit purposes.

- Identifies and protects the Gallery's vital records (i.e. those records which would be needed to re-establish the business of the Gallery in the event of a disaster, and without which it could not operate).

- Identifies and preserves securely those records deemed worthy of permanent preservation, thus protecting the Gallery's historical memory.

- Destroys other records once they are no longer required, thus ensuring the efficient use of Gallery accommodation.

- Meets relevant record-keeping requirements, including the Public Records Acts 1958 and 1967, the Freedom of Information Act 2000 etc.

6. Responsibilities

Effective Records Management is a shared responsibility.

Senior Management is responsible for approving and promoting compliance with Records Management policies and procedures, and supporting the implementation of a Records Management programme, throughout the Gallery.

The *Records Manager* is responsible for delivering the operational activities of a Records Management programme, and for the development and implementation of related procedures and guidance.

Individual members of staff are responsible for creating and maintaining records in accordance with best practice.

7. Procedures

Relevant best practice procedures can be found on the Gallery's network at the following location: xxx Practice. For advice on specific issues staff should contact the Archivist and Records Manager.

8. Breach of policy

Breaches of the Gallery's Records Management procedures will be dealt with in accordance with the Gallery's disciplinary procedure.

9. Review

The Archives and Records Management will be reviewed at least every five years (with interim reviews where necessary). The next scheduled review is July 2013.

10. Date of approval

Approved at the meeting of the Board of Trustees on 10 July 2008.

Author: Charlotte Brunskill.
Source: By kind permission of the National Portrait Gallery.

Appendix 9:
Museum record series commonly containing environmental information

Facilities/buildings and grounds
– waste (rubbish, biohazard-related, building work by-products, etc.) policies, plans and logs
– building plant plans and operational manuals
– risk assessments.

Biological collections
– environmental impact assessments
– risk assessments.

Health and safety
– incident and health reports relating to the built environment
– pest control plans, procedures and risk assessments
– COSHH files on use and disposal of chemicals used for pest control, conservation, cleaning, etc.

Appendix 10:
Records survey questionnaire forms

Direct survey questionnaire

Date:
Name:
Position:
Department:

1.   What is your/your department's official role (is there a statement in the corporate plan, for example)?

2.   What are your/your department's main functions?

3.   How many staff are in your section/department, and what are their jobs?

4.   Is there a high level of staff turnover, or have most people been in the section/department for some time?

5.   Do you have a centralised departmental filing system, or does each person maintain his/her individual system?

6.   What are the main records which support the work of the department, and how long do they need to be kept in the office? (Add data in table below.)

7.   How do you organise your e-records? Do you work mostly on the shared drive or in 'My documents'?

8.   Do other departments need access to the records managed by your department? If so, which records?

9.   Do you need access to records managed by other departments? If so, which records?

10.   Are you aware of the provisions of the Data Protection Act 1998, and do you have any related problems with your records?
        (Note any records that are covered by the DPA.)

11.   Does your department create any records concerning the environment?
        (Note any records that are covered by Environmental Information Regulations.)

12.   Do you have any obvious problems in managing your records (e.g. lack of space, volume of e-mail)?

13.   What elements of record keeping would you like to change or improve?

Details of record series

Record series title	Date of records	Retention in office	Retention in archives	Notes (legal or other factors)	Paper/ digital?	Volume

Devolved survey questionnaire

Instructions

Please complete one form per record series. Consult the Records Manager (ext. xxxx) if you have any questions about this form.

Definitions

- Record series = groups of records arranged in accordance with a filing system or managed as a unit because they relate to a particular subject or function, or result from the same activity.

- Personal data = data from which it is possible to identify a living individual.

- Vital record = records essential to the successful running of the museum in the case of disaster.

- Environmental information = information, reports, policies, plans, programmes, agreements, etc. concerning elements such as air, water, soil, land and landscapes, natural sites, coastal and marine areas and biological diversity and its components. Includes factors such as energy, noise, radiation or waste (including radioactive waste, emissions, discharges and other releases) affecting or likely to affect the elements of the environment. Also includes the state of human health and safety, the contamination of the food chain, conditions of human life, cultural sites and built structures inasmuch as they are or may be affected by the state of the elements of the environment referred to above.

- Archival value = identified for permanent preservation because the records have ongoing historical/research value to future generations.

Who is completing this form?	
1. Section/unit/department:	
2. Name of person compiling form:	
3. Date completed:	
About the records	
4. Title of record series:	
5. Description of record series: (for what purpose were they created and what information do they contain?)	
6. Date of records:	
7. Format – paper:	Loose In folders In filing cabinets On shelves In boxes Other
8. Location – paper:	Office Storage area Other

9. Format – electronic:	Word Excel PowerPoint Database E-mail Other
10. Location – electronic:	Shared drive My documents Other
11. Volume (linear metres or kilobytes/ megabytes):	
Status	
12. Do the records contain personal data? If yes, of what type?	
13. Do they contain environmental information? If yes, of what type?	
14. Do they contain confidential information? If yes, of what type?	
15. Are they vital records? If yes, of what type?	
Access and security	
16. Who should have access to the records?	

17. Are they stored securely in such a way that prevents unauthorised access?	
Retention	
18. What are the records used for?	
19. How long are the records needed?	
20. How often are the records consulted?	
21. Do the records have archival value?	
Problems	
22. Are there any problems with this record series?	
23. Is there anything you would like to change/improve about the way this record series is managed?	

Author: Charlotte Brunskill.
Source: By kind permission of the National Portrait Gallery.

Appendix 11:
Supplies checklist template

Inactive records	Archive records	General	Cost
Regular folders (ideally with no metal fasteners as they weigh more when you box up records)	Acid-free folders (no metal fasteners) for A4 and 'legal'-size documents	Pens and pencils for labelling folders	
Storage ('bankers') boxes	Acid-free storage cartons	Scissors	

Inactive records	Archive records	General	Cost
Wooden pallets to store boxes on if you do not have racking	Staple removers (scalpels)	Stable trolley for tranferring records (should hold up to six 'bankers boxes' on three lipless shelves)	
File cabinets to store records if you do not have room for boxes	Acid-free paper to use as dividers (rather than paperclips)	Shredder or access to shredder (should be able to withstand heavy use)	
Simple database to manage records (box or file inventory of records in your custody and/or records held by departments)	Separation forms for books or other published items found in archive that have been moved to other areas of the museum (you can make these yourself)	Photocopier or access to photocopier (ideally should be a 'book' copier which is easier on fragile documents)	

Inactive records	Archive records	General	Cost
Transfer forms documenting paper records moved from offices to records store (you can make these yourself)	Powder-coated (non-off-gassing) steel racking to store boxes without stacking them	Transfer or disposal forms (draft these in-house)	
		White erasers which leave no marks	
		Adequate servers/server space for 'born-digital' active, inactive and archive materials	
		Long worktable for preparing paper records for storage	

Author: Sarah R. Demb.

Appendix 12:
Sample records transfer
instruction and forms for staff

How to transfer semi-current records to the Archive

1. Introduction

The Gallery's Archive store is primarily for the storage of records which have been identified for permanent preservation. It may also be used for the storage of semi-current records where these records cannot be maintained within departments.

What are semi-current records?

Semi-current records are those records which are no longer required by the department for frequent reference, but need to be maintained in the medium term because they have ongoing financial, administrative or legal value.

What happens to the records after transfer?

Semi-current records transferred to the Archive will be processed and managed by Gallery Records staff. This means they will be assigned a retention/review period and logged on to the department's Records database.

Which semi-current records can be transferred to the Archive?

Semi-current records can only be transferred to the Archive where the transfer has been agreed with the Gallery Records staff. Records transferred must be in hard-copy (i.e. paper) format. Please do not send any records in digital format – i.e. CDs, DVDs etc. The Gallery currently has no provision for the long-term preservation of such records. If you want to retain the content of records stored in digital format you will need to print to paper and transfer the hard copy.

Can records be retrieved by departments after transfer?

Yes, once records have been transferred to the Archive they can be retrieved by departments on demand.

2. How to transfer material: what do I do?

- *Contact Gallery Records staff* – to discuss and agree details of transfer. Please do not send any unsolicited material. Records received by Gallery Records staff without prior agreement will be returned.

- *Order boxes* – semi-current records will only be accepted for transfer if they are packed into boxes supplied by Gallery Records staff (other boxes/files do not fit on

Archive shelves). Once the transfer has been agreed, you will need to estimate how many records transfer boxes you require and notify Gallery Records staff accordingly. Please do not send any material in the internal mail. Records received in this fashion will be returned.

- *Weed records* – before transferring any records to the Archive you must carry out an initial review of the material in order to weed out and destroy any material that is insignificant or ephemeral. This may include duplicates; drafts; unimportant notes/correspondence; and other records of no further value. Please note, as the creator of the records you are the best person to carry out this task.

  NB. Gallery Records staff will retain all material transferred in its entirety. A second review/weed may be carried out by Gallery Records staff at the appointed review time (see below).

- *Prepare records* – before placing in the boxes, all records should be removed from lever-arch files, ring-binders etc., and placed in cardboard folders. These can be obtained from general stationery stores. Each file should be clearly labelled, with a title that succinctly represents its contents. Gallery Records staff will check folders when processing records and will return all boxes where files have not been labelled.

- *Pack boxes* – when packing boxes, where possible only place like files in the same box, e.g. files that relate to the same activity, or are from the same record type. Packing the records in this way will help Gallery Records staff to manage the review process (see below). Do not overfill boxes as they will not fit on the shelves, can be dangerous to lift and cannot be reused. Do not secure the boxes with string or tape – if the lid does not fit properly the box is too full. *Do not write on the outside of the box.*

- *Arrange for collection of boxes* – contact Gallery Records staff who will arrange for the boxes to be collected. If you are delivering the boxes yourself, you must hand them to a member of the Gallery Records team: any boxes left in the Gallery Records work area will be returned to departments.

3. What happens to my records?

Gallery Records staff will process your transfer. This involves checking all contents; assigning a review period to the box; recording relevant details on to the Records database; and physically transferring the boxes to the basement.

Assigning action and review periods

- Following an initial weed by creating departments, all semi-current records transferred to the Archive must be assigned a second review period.

- Second review periods are assigned at box level and take the following format: action, number of years, e.g. Review +6.

  - In relation to the above, action equals either destroy, review or transfer to Archive.

  - The number of years determines when the action will take place. In most cases this will be +6, in accordance with the Limitations Act, 1980.

- The action and review periods are assigned by Gallery Records staff, taking into account the ongoing legal, financial, historical and administrative value of the particular type of record transferred.

- The action and review periods for some record types are well established. This tends to be the case where departments have a strong tradition of regularly transferring material (e.g. exhibition case files).

- If your department does not regularly transfer material, or the type of records contained in the particular transfer is completely new, then an action and review period needs to be established following consultation with Gallery Records staff.

Managing action and review periods

- The second review and weeding process will take place in accordance with the review period assigned to the records on transfer (see above). This process will be undertaken solely by Gallery Records staff.

- You will be notified of any records identified for destruction. If, for any reason, you wish to retain the records for a further period you will need to discuss this with Gallery Records staff.

- You will not be notified about records which have been reviewed and will be transferred to the Archive for permanent preservation. Such records will be catalogued on to the historical records database (CALM) and made readily available to staff and the public.

4. How do I recall my records if I need to consult them?

- Any semi-current records transferred to the Archive can be recalled by departments at any time. Please contact Gallery Records staff who will aim, where possible, to offer a same-day service.

- Retrieval requests should be directed to Gallery Records staff only. Other staff in the Archive and Library department have no dealings with these records.

Author: Charlotte Brunskill.
Source: By kind permission of the National Portrait Gallery.

Records Transfer /Disposal Form

Name: **Date:**

Department:

Records to be transferred or destroyed [strike out as necessary]

Title / **description** / **format** of records – [Department] Records:

Date range of records: yyyy-yyyy or M-M YYYY

Quantity of records [metres or boxes]:

Agreement [strike out as appropriate]:

I hereby state that the records described above are no longer required by the Museum.
I hereby state that the records described above are required by the Museum until a specified destruction date.
I hereby state that the records described above are no longer required by the Museum over the long term.

Name, Head of Department

_____Signature   _____Date

Authorisation Signature
_____ (Museum Records Manager)

NAME

_____ Date

Source: By kind permission of the Museum of London.

References

Collections Trust (2008) *SPECTRUM*, 3rd edn; available at: *www.collectionslink.org.uk/manage-information/ spectrum* (accessed: 31 March 2010).

Cook, Michael (1984) *Manual of Archival Description*. Liverpool: University of Liverpool.

Government of the Northwest Territories, Canada (2002) *Records Management Bulletin*, No. 6; available at: *www. pws.gov.nt.ca/pdf/recordsManagement/bulletins/ PDFBulletin_06.pdf* (accessed: 31 December 2010).

Information Commissioner's Office (undated.a) 'Freedom of Information and Environmental Information Regulations: Hints for practitioners answering FOI and EIR requests'; available at: *www.ico.gov.uk/upload/documents/library/ freedom_of_information/practical_application/foi_hints_ for_practitioners_handing_foi_and_eir_requests_2008_ final.pdf* (accessed: 31 December 2010).

Information Commissioner's Office (undated.b) 'Routinely publishing environmental information'; available at: *www. ico.gov.uk/~/media/documents/library/Environmental_ info_reg/Practical_application/PROACTIVE DISSEMINATION.ashx* (accessed: 31 December 2010).

JISC (undated) 'InfoKit on risk management'; available at *www.jiscinfonet.ac.uk* (accessed: 28 November 2010).

National Museum Directors Conference (1998) 'UK museums' provenance research for the period 1933–1945:

statement of principles and proposed actions'; available at: *www.nationalmuseums.org.uk/activities/spoliation/ spoliation_statement/* (accessed: 31 March 2010).

Pearce-Moses, Richard (2005) *A Glossary of Archival and Records Terminology*. Chicago, IL: Society of American Archivists.

SCAM (2003) 'Information Sheet 5: Managing a museum's administrative records', Standing Conference on Archives in Museums; available at: *www.archivesandmuseums.org. uk/scam/Infosheet5.htm* (accessed: 31 December 2010).

Taylor, Brandon (1999) *Art for the Nation: Exhibitions and the London Public, 1747–2001*. Manchester: Manchester University Press.

The National Archives (1999) 'What is a public record? Summary guidance note for places of deposit'; available at: *https://www.nationalarchives.gov.uk/documents/what isapublicrecord.pdf* (accessed: 10 December 2010).

Wythe, Deborah (ed.) (2004) *Museum Archives: An Introduction*. Chicago, IL: Society of American Archivists.

Index